HILDEGARD

HILDEGARD

PROPHET OF
THE COSMIC CHRIST

═══ ✛ ═══

Renate Craine

A Crossroad Book
The Crossroad Publishing Company
New York

1997

The Crossroad Publishing Company
370 Lexington Avenue, New York, NY 10017

Copyright © 1997 by Renate Craine

Printed in the United States of America

For acknowledgments of previously published material, please see p. 12,
which constitutes an extension of the copyright page.

Library of Congress Cataloging-in-Publication Data

Craine, Renate.
    Hildegard : prophet of the cosmic Christ / Renate Craine.
      p.   cm. — (The Crossroad spiritual legacy series)
    Includes bibliographical references.
    ISBN 0-8245-2510-8 (pbk.)
    1. Hildegard, Saint, 1098–1179.   I. Title. II. Series.
BX4700.H5C73 1997
282'.092–dc21   97–14702

For Jim

Through the fountain-fullness of the Word came the embrace of God's maternal love, which nourishes us into life, is our help in perils, and — as a most profound and gentle love—opens us for repentance.

—HILDEGARD OF BINGEN, *Scivias* II, 2, 4

Contents

List of Illustrations

Abbreviations

BR   *Briefwechsel*

CB/LS   *Cecelia Bonn/Leben als Spannungseinheit*

CC   *Causae et curae*

DL   *Das Leben der heiligen Hildegard von Bingen*

DR   Dronke, *Women Writers of the Middle Ages*

DW   *Liber divinorum operum* (The Book of Divine Works) (entitled *De operatione Dei* in the oldest codex [1170–73])

HK   *Heilkunde*

HW   *Heilwissen*

L   *The Letters of Hildegard of Bingen*, vol. 1

MV   *Der Mensch in der Verantwortung* (*Liber vitae meritorum*)

PI   J. P. Pitra, ed., *Analecta S. Hildegardis*, vol. 8 of *Analecta sacra*

RB   The Rule of St. Benedict

SC   *Scivias*

SY   *Symphonia*

WM   *Welt und Mensch* (*De operatione Dei*)

Unless otherwise noted, English translations of Hildegard's writings are the author's own. References to Hildegard's works are to book, vision, and chapter; for example, SC III, 10, 31 = *Scivias*, book 3, vision 10, chapter 31.

Acknowledgments

To all those who have encouraged my search for Hildegard's wisdom I give thanks:

To Sr. Caecilia Bonn, OSB, who guided me high into the great tree of Hildegard's symbolic thought and generously shared time and insights with me. To Sr. Adelgundis Führkötter, OSB, who years ago encouraged my research on Hildegard. To the sisters at the Abtei St. Hildegard for their scholarship, critical editions, translations, and their Benedictine hospitality.

To women companions on the journey who fed my spirit, shared, and encouraged me to write — Kathleen O'Connor; Miriam Perlewitz, MM; Janet Ruffing, SM; Ann Sturges; Lucille Naughton; Polly Wiley; Jo Maloney; Bea Newman; Fredericka Cutler; and my daughter Renate.

To Grace Meyerjack, MM, and Robin van Loeben Sels, who guided me to still-points of discernment. To Henri Nouwen, whose words and example, while he walked among us, have been true gift and an apprenticeship in being "beloved of God."

To teachers whose intellectual rigor and fidelity to their own call illuminated different facets of the Divine Mystery for me — Bill Frazier, MM; and Larry Lewis, MM, both at the Maryknoll School of Theology; Beth Johnson and Ewert Cousins at Fordham University; and Caroline Walker Bynum at Columbia University.

For difficulties encountered on the journey that helped me to find my voice.

To my students and fellow searchers in the "Guild for Spiritual Guidance," whose faith, insights, and struggles continue to reveal the abiding presence of the "Living Light" in all things.

To Lynn Schmitt Quinn, my editor, who mothered the writing of this book with encouragement and wisdom.

To my children and grandchildren for their love, understanding, laughter, and care, which make my life so rich.

✤

The author and publisher wish to thank the following for permission to include previously published material (the following information constitutes an extension of the copyright page):

From *RB 1980, The Rule of St. Benedict*, copyright © 1981 by The Order of St. Benedict, Inc. Published by The Liturgical Press, Collegeville, Minnesota. Used with permission.

From *Hildegard of Bingen: Mystical Writings*. Edited and introduced by Fiona Bowie and Oliver Davies with new translations by Robert Carver. Introduction and compilation © 1990 by Fiona Bowie and Oliver Davies. Robert Carver's translations © by Robert Carver. The Crossroad Spiritual Classics Series. (New York: Crossroad, 1993). Used with permission of The Crossroad Publishing Company and SPCK.

From *Women Writers of the Middle Ages*, edited and translated by Peter Dronke. Cambridge: Cambridge University Press, 1984. Reprinted with permission of Cambridge University Press.

From St. Hildegard of Bingen: *Symphonia: A Critical Edition of the Symphonia armonie celestium revelationum*. Edited and translated by Barbara Newman. Copyright © 1989 by Cornell University. Used by permission of the publisher, Cornell University Press.

Special thanks to Otto Müller Verlag, KG, for permission to reproduce six illuminations from the illustrated Rupertsberg codex of *Scivias I* and *Scivias II* and the illustrated Lucca manuscript of *De operatione Dei*, and for permission to translate from their editions of *Hildegard von Bingen, Briefwechsel*. Nach den ältesten Handschriften übersetzt und nach den Quellen erläutert von Adelgundis Führkötter, OSB. (Salzburg: Otto Müller Verlag, 1965); *Das Leben der heiligen Hildegard von Bingen*. Ein Bericht aus dem 12. Jahrhundert verfasst von den Mönchen Gottfried und Theoderich. Aus dem Lateinischen übersetzt und kommentiert von Adelgundis Führkötter (Salzburg: Otto Müller Verlag, 1980); and *Hildegard von Bingen, Der Mensch in der Verantworung*. Das Buch der Lebensverdienste (LIBER VITAE MERITORUM) Nach den Quellen übersetzt und erläutert von Heinrich Schipperges. (Salzburg: Otto Müller Verlag, 1972).

From *The Letters of Hildegard of Bingen*, vol 1., edited by Joseph L. Baird and Radd K. Ehrman, translated by Joseph L. Baird and Radd K. Ehrman. Translation copyright © 1994 by Joseph L. Baird and Radd K. Ehrman. Used by permission of Oxford University Press.

Foreword

Writing in the fourth century a North African Christian by the name of Lactantius offered the following definition of virtue. For him, virtue is nothing less than "enduring of evils and labors." How unlike contemporary notions this definition of virtue is and how odd it sounds for us to be told so plainly that the fullness of life can be had only through enduring evils and trials. Yet, despite our inclination to write off Lactantius as an overly pessimistic nay-sayer, we must admit that life does include a large dose of suffering. We can take it well or badly. We can flee it or embrace it, but it will come and find us wherever we hide, and then it will test our mettle. Virtue does involve suffering evils, not simply actualizing ourselves, or conquering our fears, or visualizing success, or learning techniques to cope with stress, or building better "relationships" with members of the opposite sex. There are things in life that simply cannot be so easily manipulated. Situations that don't get better. Unpleasant realities that won't go away. Where do we turn when confronted by them?

We can turn to the externals, to our comforts and our conveniences, to the superficialities of our lives, or we can turn to our depths. Many who have lived before us have learned the hard way that turning to the depths is the way to a fuller life. Their insights have been handed down, often in forms that are now hard to find and harder to read. Their language is archaic. Their morality out of sync with ours. Their clarity, off-putting. Their humility, disconcerting. Yet they are there, waiting quietly to share with us their hard-won wisdom, waiting to dialog with us as we face situations that are different from those they encountered only in the particulars, not in the essences.

Simply put, that is the reason why Crossroad, myself, and a team of well-known scholars and spiritual leaders have joined together to undertake the Spiritual Legacy series. The need for spiritual wisdom is great. Our situation is critical. This then is more than an enterprise in scholarship, more than a literary exercise. It is an effort to convey life.

Certainly the idea of doing editions of the works of spiritual guides from the past is not new. There are a host of books available that do just that. How is the Spiritual Legacy series different?

The uniqueness of this series abides in its content and its style. In content it endeavors to present both texts from the spiritual guide and extensive commentary by a present-day disciple of the sage. It gives the reader the chance to encounter for herself the writings of a spiritual master. Nothing can take the place of that experience. However demanding it might be, whatever efforts it might require, there can be no substitute for it. One, for instance, cannot simply hear a description of the tenth chapter of Augustine's *Confessions*. No commentary, however skilled, can take the place of reading for oneself Augustine's words of unparalleled power: "Late have I loved Thee, O Beauty, so ancient, yet so new!"

While it is true that there is no substitute for encountering the text firsthand, it is also certain that for most people that encounter will be an excursion into a foreign land. Often many centuries and numerous barriers of language, customs, philosophy, and style separate us from the writings of bygone sages. To come to that point where we can understand the horizon of the author, we must be taught something about the historical context, the literary style, and the thought forms of the age, for instance. That is why we have included in this series extensive commentary on the text. That commentary is alternated with the text throughout the books, so that one can be taught, then experience the writings firsthand, over and over as one moves deeper into the text. At that point, the horizon of the reader meets that of the author, aided by the expert guidance of the editor of each book, who suggests not only what the text might mean, but how it might be made part of our lives.

The style of the Spiritual Legacy series is also unique in that it attempts to convey life with a certain degree of sophistication that befits an educated readership. Yet it does not assume that everyone will have a background in the material presented, nor does it purport to offer original or arcane scholarship. The editors' mastery of the texts is in each case complemented by their experience in putting the meaning of the texts into practice and helping others to do so as well. We are trying to present a series of books that will fit somewhere between the scholarly editions that pride themselves on their accuracy and originality and the popular pieces that offer too little substance for the healthy reader.

The series is designed to be used by a broad range of people. For those seekers who wish to journey toward spiritual wholeness as part of a group, the series is ideally suited. The texts presented can be easily divided into sections for discussion by a group meeting, say, on a weekly basis.

For those who are traveling alone, the series is a trustworthy and enjoyable tour book. The direct, simple language of the commentaries frames the memorable words of the classical texts and offers them in an attractive setting for meditation and practical application.

The publisher and editors of the Spiritual Legacy series join me in inviting you to undertake a journey that will take you back to an encounter with ancient wisdom and challenge you to an experience of self-understanding and, at its best, self-transcendence. It is our hope that that experience will help you to grow and to be a source of fresh life for all those around you.

John Farina

Preface

Hildegard of Bingen, Wisdom's Prophet

I now speak from Scripture through a person who is not ready to speak, through one who is not taught by a human teacher. I, Who Am, proclaim through her new secrets and mystical truth hidden up to now in books, like a person who first mixes clay and then decides what shapes to form. (SC III, 11, 18)

These bold words were proclaimed by a woman who, as reluctantly as the prophets of old, had at last acknowledged her call and task. A profound prophetic vision opened the great depth of Scripture's meaning and told her to write the things she saw and heard. The "food of life of divine Scripture" became the food for her life. Only gradually and reluctantly did Hildegard of Bingen accept God's invitation to speak, challenge, and console in God's name.

From the time of her call, at the age of forty-three, she cooperated with God's grace by writing, dictating, and composing liturgical music, by investigating natural science, medicine, and herbal remedies, by guiding the illuminators of her visions, and by venturing into the public arena. Her contemporaries listened to the "German prophetess," as they called her. Powerful leaders, monks, and simple people asked her advice and counsel about spiritual and personal matters and about political, ecclesial, and even theological controversies.

Speaking to us across the centuries, Hildegard writes not about personal mystical union but rather about the Mystery of God, who in Christ is present in the cosmos, in history, and in the depth of our hearts. She writes about the realm of

17

divine human encounter, about Divine Wisdom, God's partner and companion in history. Hildegard reminds us who we
truly are before we put on the many faces we wear. We are
not determined by the past, by habits, by conditioning, by
circumstances; they are only the clothing hung on the mystery of our being. She reminds us that human beings have
inherent dignity, and she evokes for us what it means to be
human in a cosmos that is meant to reveal the Divine Mystery.
When our hearts are transformed in Christ, when the earth becomes sanctified by wise human choice, then our hearts become
God's dwelling place, she tells us. For "through the fountain-
fullness of the Word came the embrace of God's maternal love,
which nourishes us into life, is our help in perils, and — as a
most profound and gentle love — opens us for repentance" (SC
II, 2, 4).

We somehow have to cross the centuries if we are to understand her complex texts. God's revelations to Hildegard were
shaped into words and images within a concrete, historical context, yet they contain a core of transcultural wisdom that invites
translation into the language and consciousness of our age. My
own emphasis and specific selections of texts arise from my
contemporary assumptions and my struggle to find God in all
of life today as well as in the wisdom of tradition.

Over the years Hildegard's words, images, music, and life
have become a source of delight, ambiguity, hope, and challenge for me. I have discovered three bridges that helped me
to cross the abyss of the centuries and to hear "with the ears
of my heart," as Hildegard would call it, not only with ears
conditioned by modes of modern concerns and scholarship. Perhaps these three bridges into Hildegard's complex texts will be
helpful to other modern readers:

1. Hildegard's choice of symbolic, archetypal language;

2. her Benedictine spirituality as focus and influence; and

3. the female experience as filter and lens.

Each bridge leads to a specific perspective on the Divine Mystery, conveying in some unique way the experience of God and
its expression. As you read the pages that follow, you might
gradually notice that each bridge leads below the surface of life,

leads to the realm where grace and fecundity are the hidden potential in a complex, incomplete, but ultimately sacramental universe.

Hildegard, Wisdom's prophet, can become a mentor for both the personal and the communal journey as we face reality at the dawn of the twenty-first century. Her life is an example of the transformative, challenging power of God and of the human ability to respond. Her words and the symbolic images of the great story she tells provide a magnificent framework for perceiving the hidden radiance of Love within a world torn by conflict and division, then and now.

Chapter 1

Hildegard's Life and Work

Hildegard of Bingen was an extraordinary figure in the tumultuous times of the twelfth century. As abbess, physician, prophet, theologian, writer, and composer, she had great impact on her age. She counseled many individuals and involved herself in the political struggles of both church and empire with a boldness that was rooted in her prophetic task. She called people out of forgetfulness of God and into the tension of their God-given historical responsibility. Her contemporaries revered Hildegard and listened to this passionate woman who spoke about herself as a "poor little female" who desired to be "a feather on the breath of God," yet claimed God-given authority for her words and involvements. She was at home in the healing arts as well as in agriculture. She knew about the power of precious stones, and she was so knowledgeable about fish that she surprises modern ichthyologists. She composed seventy liturgical songs and wrote books about theology, ethics, and cosmology. Hildegard corresponded with the high and mighty in church and state, with abbots, simple nuns, and laypeople. Her visionary words and images challenged her listeners and readers with a consciousness that called them beyond the cultural and religious consciousness of their era. She continues to challenge modern readers.

All but forgotten for eight hundred years, Hildegard's relational worldview and theology have been rediscovered in the twentieth century. Learned Benedictine nuns in Germany have been influential in researching, translating, and publishing Hildegard's works. Hildegard emerges as a woman of amazing actuality whose achievements interest not only scholars in a variety of fields but also spiritual searchers far and wide. Scholarly and popular books in English are slowly catching up with her popularity in the German-speaking world, where books, symposia, television shows, pharmacies selling her remedies, and Jubilee years celebrating her have long publicized her importance for our age. The German bishops even petitioned Rome to have her declared a "Doctor of the Church," the third woman after Teresa of Àvila and Catherine of Sienna to be considered for that high distinction. Popular devotion, however, never needed official recognition.

Hildegard filtered her experiences of the Mystery of God through the consciousness of her time in history. To discover her transcultural message we somehow have to translate it for men and women whose modern consciousness and mentality are very different from that of the twelfth century. We need bridges that help us cross the abyss that separates our worlds. But we also need to discover that our deepest longings resonate with Hildegard's own longings and her resulting involvements.

Hildegard was born in the summer of 1098 in Bermersheim near the old Roman fortification of Alzey, about twelve miles from the cathedral city of Mainz. She was the tenth child of Hiltebert von Bermersheim and his wife, Mechthild, who were part of the local nobility. Hildegard thus grew up in an extended family of wealth and connections. She was born into a century of tremendous conflicts, change, and religious restlessness. It was a time of population growth and expansion, of dramatic weather changes and resulting poor harvests. Recovering from the barbarian invasions, nation-states formed, agricultural productivity increased, commerce flourished, trade routes linked all of Europe, and cities grew in wealth and importance. A new era of learning took its place beside the monastic culture of teaching the desire for God. Urban cathedral schools, many of which later became universities, prepared clerics whose goal was the acquisition of knowledge. Newly recovered writings of Aristotle were translated from Arabic into Latin, and crusaders left for Jerusalem. Churches and cathedrals sprang up, most of them dedicated to Mary. There were attempts to reform a church that had become tainted by simony and self-indulgence, among them a variety of new spiritual reform movements. Popes and emperors were involved in bitter controversies that produced decades of localized civil wars. Each claimed to be the true representative of God for this world. Each claimed to have the right to invest bishops with both temporal and spiritual powers. What sets Hildegard's century apart from our age of conflict and change is a social and religious structure within which every person knew his or her place in life as having been preordained by God.

From early childhood on, Hildegard had visionary experiences we would now describe as mystical, clairvoyant, or paranormal. Assuming that everybody "saw" as she did, she confided in her nurse and found out that others did not have these experiences. She then concealed the power and mystery of her visions, but they continued, shaking her to the depth of her being.

Following the custom of noble families, Hildegard's parents gave their tenth child to God as a tithe when she was eight years old. They made a radical choice when they gave their child into the care of an anchoress, rather than giving her as an oblate to a convent. How serious a step this was becomes apparent when one looks at the solemn liturgical rite performed by a bishop at the enclosure ceremony for an anchoress, a rite that symbolized dying to the world and rising with Christ. The anchoress was given extreme unction and was sprinkled with dust or ashes before she entered her "grave," the anchorhold, whose entrance was then sealed. Hildegard's parents entrusted her care and education to the noblewoman Jutta von Spanheim, who lived as a recluse in an anchorage that was attached to the thriving Benedictine monastery of Disibodenberg. Jutta educated Hildegard and some other young women in the monastic way of life. The anchorage had a window that opened into the adjoining church so that the anchoress and her charges could listen to the monks' chanting of the Divine Office, the *opus Dei*, and could participate in the Eucharist. Local people came to the anchorage and spoke to Jutta through another window to get advice and counsel. Servants, priests, or doctors were able to enter through an unsealed door.

We moderns ask, Why would one put a child into such an enclosure? For one thing it was not unusual to tithe a tenth child to God, just as one would tithe a tenth of the harvest. But another reason to give this child into the safety of an anchorhold might have been fear — fear of the child's unusual visionary gifts and of her future. It was an age when healing powers and direct access to God were questioned. The role of wise women, midwives, healers, and counselors became dangerous business. Their practice of perceiving the sacred in all of nature was gradually questioned and eventually condemned by church authorities. Witch trials by the Inquisition in the following centuries resulted in a veritable holocaust of women. Were Hildegard's parents aware of danger for their child? We don't know, but surely Jutta was an inspired choice.

Jutta must have been a woman of extraordinary spiritual gifts, a *magistra* who attracted a wide circle of disciples. Jutta, Hildegard, and their servant were gradually joined by others, so that by 1113 the anchorhold had become a small Benedictine convent, attached to the adjoining monastery and dependent on the monks for liturgical and administrative services. Jutta introduced Hildegard and the other women to the Rule of St. Benedict and to life shaped by its spirit. She instructed them in Holy Scripture and in chanting the Psalms in Latin. Life according to the Rule of St. Benedict balanced prayer with work and strove for discernment, *discretio,* in all situations.

Her *Vita,* the story of Hildegard's life that was completed shortly after her death, tells us that she received no formal instruction in reading or in music. Her instruction differed from the instruction of the monks in the famous monastery schools; it differed from training in the cathedral schools; and it most certainly differed from instruction in the newly developing universities. Compared with accepted standards of education, hers was rudimentary. She herself tells us that she selected a teacher from whom she received instruction and advice, the monk Volmar of Disibodenberg. He was more than a teacher, spiritual director, and confessor. Hildegard not only learned how to plumb the depths of Scripture but also how to treasure the works, or at least the ideas, of the Fathers of the Church and of medieval authors. This was most unusual for a woman. Volmar, the learned monk, gradually gave up the teacher's role to sit at the feet of his former pupil. He was to become her secretary, trusted helper, and friend, a confidant who knew and trusted her visionary gifts.

At the age of sixteen Hildegard freely chose to make her

monastic profession. When Jutta died in 1136, Hildegard was elected to become abbess, or spiritual mother, of the small convent. Having lived in total seclusion for more than thirty years, Hildegard was nevertheless aware of the problems of the times. Abbesses, especially those of noble birth, were actively involved in many aspects of the world, for they had feudal ties and obligations. They functioned as trusted advisers not only to the powerful in state and church but also — in Hildegard's case — to those who brought their concerns to the anchorage window. The nuns also had contacts with the monks. Hildegard observed the continuous building activity and expansion of the Disibodenberg monastery. The monks built an enormous new church and a large new monastery that included an infirmary and a guest house. Exposure to this expansion probably helped Hildegard with the details and problems of building her own convent in years to come. On a deeper level we can assume that it influenced her use of building symbolism in her written works.

For decades Hildegard lived monastic life like any other nun, even when she became abbess. She had hidden the unrelenting burden of her visionary gifts from everyone except Jutta and Volmar. Although visions were a socially sanctioned activity for women in religious life only, giving them power to speak publicly from their experience, Hildegard worried. She was afraid of self-deception, afraid to speak out as a visionary whose visions were not subjective revelations but instead vehicles for objective theological content that were directed to the church at large. She was afraid of the judgment of others. Fear held her prisoner for almost forty vision-studded years until she received her prophetic call vision and was awakened to a profound new level of her identity as a woman whom God had called to total identification with all of God's people and all of creation. Hildegard tells us how she focused her attention toward a heavenly vision of a fiery brilliance. Out of this fire a voice told her, fragile human being that she was, to speak out and to write down what she saw and heard.

She still hesitated to write, even though Volmar, whom she consulted, urged her to follow God's demand. She fell ill and wrestled with the Mystery of God, whom she experienced not only as the Living Light but also as dark and zealous, challenging her to deepen her trust in God and in herself. When she finally started to write, the illness lifted and she gradually, over many years, became aware of the imprint of the Son of Man on her consciousness. She became aware of herself as a woman who was called to become fruitful in discernment, words, and action. In the process of writing, she became aware of herself as a woman who was called to be Wisdom's prophet in an "effeminate," lukewarm age that lacked faith-filled leadership. As a woman whose self-identity was deeply affirmed by God, she felt compelled to call others to that deep interior transformation that results in the courage to confront all self-deceptive systems of unrelatedness, both personal and communal.

She worked for ten years on *Scivias* (Know the ways of God), trying to put visionary imagery and audition into human language. Self-doubt still haunted her, but she had the support of two faithful assistants: Volmar and the nun Richardis von Stade. We find that the word "I" disappeared from her writings as she consented to become a "feather on the breath of God." In 1146–47, she wrote to the challenger and confidant of emperors and popes, Bernard of Clairvaux, asking whether she should speak openly or remain silent about her visions, which were a great burden. Bernard acknowledged her charism and implored her to embrace it. Bernard was important, but his judgment was not enough for Hildegard. She felt the need to have her prophetic call legitimized by the official church. After all, her books were theological and dealt with the most profound Christian doctrines. The process of legitimation started with Volmar and the abbot of Disibodenberg, who then informed the diocese of Mainz, which in turn sent a commission to her convent to examine the evidence. Final approval of her prophetic charism was given by the Cistercian Pope Eugenius III at the synod in Trier in 1147–48. Bernard of Clairvaux and the archbishop of Mainz had sent a partial copy of *Scivias* to the pope and had intervened on her behalf. An extraordinary thing happened as a result: the pope read aloud to the assembled bishops from this book by a woman. All the bishops applauded when Bernard urged the pope to "not allow such a brilliant light to be covered by silence but rather to confirm this charism through his authority." The pope consequently wrote to Hildegard, encouraging her in the name of Christ and of St. Peter to make known all that was revealed to her in the Holy Spirit; he practically ordered her to write.

It took ten years to finish *Scivias,* her first visionary book, which deals with the creative and redemptive power of a triune God who enables our response. She did not dictate it, but wrote it herself on a wax tablet. She wrote in Latin, the language of the liturgy, of Scripture, and of learned male theologians, rather than in her German mother tongue. She had learned Latin by hearing Scripture and the Psalms in the language, through a kind of Berlitz method. Correct grammatical construction was not part of it. In later centuries it was sometimes asked how her prophesies could be of the Holy Spirit if her grammar was so inexact! Her use of Latin gives us an insight into her intended audience and also into her growing self-confidence as a woman called to be a prophet by God who "uses the weak to confound the strong."

Hildegard's fame as a holy woman was spreading and attracting many new postulants. The accommodations of the small convent were soon stretched to capacity. One day Hildegard announced that God had commanded her in a vision to establish an independent convent on the Rupertsberg, a mountain near Bingen. It is located some nineteen miles from the Disibodenberg monastery. In spite of strong resistance from Abbot Kuno and his monks, who did not want the famous abbess to leave, and in spite of the grumbling of her own sisters, who preferred the comfort of the old convent, Hildegard prevailed. The abbot came to believe that the severe illness and paralysis Hildegard suffered when he objected to her plan was sent by God and would not lift until she followed God's will. The abbot finally allowed her to proceed.

We come to know Hildegard as a very astute woman of great ability and independence in this episode. Through the Marchioness Richardis von Stade, the mother of one of her nuns, Hildegard had gained influence with the Archbishop of Mainz and had obtained financial support to buy the property. She moved with eighteen nuns to the new convent and was able to convince the abbot that the land given by relatives of her nuns was not part of his monastery but belonged to the new foundation. The archbishop drew up a legal separation between Hildegard's convent and the Disibodenberg monastery.

This document established the respective rights and obligations of the Benedictine monastery and of Hildegard's new and independent foundation on the Rupertsberg. Her convent was granted the right to freely elect its own abbesses and to retain the services of the monks solely for liturgical and administrative assistance. Hildegard's arrangements were carefully crafted with the intention that the nuns would have allegiance to no one but God and the archbishop and would be free from obligations to any prince or landowner.

The little girl who had entered the anchorhold had become a strong, independent leader in whom the buried power of the feminine rose in incredible ways, almost despite her culture and conditioning. Difficulties with her nuns occurred over privations they all suffered in their first few years in Rupertsberg, but they were also a result of the departure of her favorite nun and helper, Richardis von Stade, who was to become abbess at Bassum. Stunned by what she felt as betrayal and deep loss, Hildegard used any means and all her power to prevent this move. She did not succeed in this, but she did become conscious that her own desires had a dark side. In 1165, as the Rupertsberg convent expanded, she founded a sister-convent in Eibingen on the other side of the Rhine, which she visited twice a week.

She became a model abbess. She opened a hospice, installed running water and a sewage system, and counseled many people wisely. During this time Hildegard wrote many of her hymns and sequences as well as her medical and scientific books. Between 1158 and 1163 she wrote a second visionary book on ethics, *Liber vitae meritorum* (The Book of Life's Merits), in which she shows the opposing forces that mold human ethical behavior. It is not an abstract book on moral theology, but rather a symbolic conversation between the thirty-five powers of God she calls virtues, which oppose an equal number of vices. It gives evidence of her experience with people and her insight into their deepest desires and defenses. This perception had its roots in the depth of her God-consciousness.

Her third visionary book, *De operatione Dei* (The Book of Divine Works), was written between 1163 and 1174. It is a cosmology in which she shows humanity and creation as most intimately related to God and to each other. In this worldview the microcosm reveals the macrocosm, and all of history is salvation history. Hildegard also wrote a book of natural history (*Physica*), a medical book (*Causae et curae*), commentaries on the Rule of St. Benedict and the Creed, and biographies of St. Disibod and St. Rupert. The seventy-seven liturgical songs she wrote and composed are collected in *Symphonia harmoniae caelestium revelationum* (Symphony of the Harmony of Celestial Revelations).

Hildegard's correspondence gives evidence of her wide influence. She was in contact with popes, queens and emperors, abbesses and abbots, nuns and monks, and a variety of laypeople. Her correspondence spans not only Germany but also Denmark, England, France, Italy, and Greece. In her letters to different popes she describes herself repeatedly as "a feather on the breath of God," and from this consciousness she openly confronts them. For instance, she tells Pope Anastasius IV to "wake up from the slumber of tolerance and fatigue in discernment." She corresponded with bishops and archbishops and responded with admirable depth and clarity when Magister Odo of Paris and Bishop Eberhard II of Bamberg asked her for theological opinions. Some of the most fascinating letters to royalty are those written to Emperor Frederick I in Germany, who was called Barbarossa, "red beard." In an effort to consolidate his power he had assumed the right to nominate bishops and to count on their loyalty. In 1159, trying to universalize his power, the emperor declared the pope deposed and proceeded to nominate three consecutive counterpopes. Hildegard, who had met Barbarossa, at first remained neutral in this schism, which was to last eighteen years. However, when the emperor named the second counterpope, Hildegard confronted him. In her eyes he had become an enemy of the Kingdom of God. She wrote to him: "O king, it is of utmost necessity that you take care how you act. In the mysterious vision, I see you acting like a child. You live an insane, absurd life before God. There is still time" (BR 86).

The emperor did not reply. Hildegard continued to challenge him. Her words sound unusual to modern ears, but they witness to an extraordinary fact. A "simple" nun in the twelfth century confronted an emperor and became involved in politics because she was so keenly aware of personal and political pathologies that opposed the human potential for interrelations reflective of the Kingdom of God.

She suffered another illness for almost three years, yet felt urged by the Holy Spirit to undertake four extensive preaching tours in order to call monasteries and the clergy to conversion. She was now in her sixties. In Cologne she preached against the threat of the Cathars, a dualist movement whose influence (she thought) was undermining the Christian worldview. Hildegard saw the danger, warned the faithful, and scolded the clergy for not preaching and living the true Gospel. We know what she said because the dean of the cathedral and the clergy wrote her to ask for a copy of her powerful homily, which starts:

> "The one who was, and is, and is about to come" (Apoc. 1:4) speaks to the shepherds of the Church:...
>
> I set you like the sun and the other luminaries so you might bring light to people through the fire of doctrine, shining in good reputation, and setting hearts ablaze with zeal....
>
> But your tongues are silent, failing to join in with the mighty voice of the resounding trumpet of the Lord, for you do not love holy reason, which, like the stars, holds the circuit of its orbit. The trumpet of the Lord is the justice of God, which you should meditate upon zealously in holiness, and through the law and obedience of your office make it known to the people at the proper time with holy discretion, rather than pounding them mercilessly with it.
>
> But you are not doing this on account of the waywardness of your own will. Thus the luminaries are missing from the firmament of God's justice in your utterances, as when the stars do not shine, for you are the night exhaling darkness, and you are like people who do not work, nor even walk in the light because of your indolence. But just as a snake hides in a cave after it has shed its skin, you walk in filth like disgusting beasts! (L 55–56)

In 1173 her friend and secretary, Volmar, died. Gottfried, monk of Disibodenberg, became her new secretary and provost. At his death in 1176, Wibert of Gembloux, whose prior correspondence with Hildegard gives us the often-quoted description of Hildegard's visionary mode, became her secretary.

Hildegard's last years were overshadowed by a painful controversy. A nobleman who had been excommunicated went to confession and Communion in her church and was subsequently buried in the convent cemetery. The ecclesial authorities at Mainz ordered her to remove his body from sacred ground and to bury him somewhere else. Convinced that this man was reconciled with his God, she refused, and she defiantly wielded her abbess's crook, leveling all the graves. An Interdict was pronounced that prohibited all liturgical services at Rupertsberg, a hard and bitter punishment for Hildegard and her nuns, for whom the Eucharist and the *opus Dei* were the highest forms of praise and adoration. Hildegard confronted the pope and prelates, complaining about the enforced silence and the injustice to the deceased. Shortly before her death her assessment of the situation was accepted, but proof of the nobleman's absolution needed to be established through the testimony of trustworthy men. The Interdict was revoked. Living out of the strength and empowerment of her prophetic visions, Hildegard walked her difficult and unusual journey with God and his people. She died on September 17, 1179, at the age of eighty-one.

Official canonization eluded this charismatic woman, although she seems to have slipped in through the backdoor. In the sixteenth century we — surprisingly — find her included in the *Roman Martyrology* of Baronius. In monastic circles and among the faithful in Germany there was never any doubt about her sainthood. Her cult flourished, and her shrine, which bears the inscription, "Holy Hildegard, pray for us," is revered. In 1979, at a celebration commemorating the eight hundredth anniversary of her death, the German bishops sent a request to Rome to have her declared a "Doctor of the Church."

Chapter 2

"Cry Out and Tell What Is Shown to You"

Arise, therefore, cry out and tell what is shown to you by the strong power of God's help. God who rules all of creation with power and mercy floods those who fear Him and serve Him in joyous love and humility with the light of celestial illumination. He guides those who persevere in the way of justice to the joys of eternal vision. (SC I, 1)

Prophetic Authority

Led by the Spirit and gradually shedding fear and illusions, Hildegard presents us with a map of the far regions where God's Spirit and the human spirit meet. Their union brings forth fecundity under the impact of God's Love and lets Wisdom make her home among human beings on earth.

Let us look at Hildegard's visions and illuminations from two perspectives to see what Hildegard tells us about these far regions. What does she report about the Mystery of God? How does she do theology from her perspective of being a woman? What does Hildegard tell us about the spiritual journey when she sees fecundity (*viriditas*) and aridity (*ariditas*) as the polarities within which the spiritual life moves?

The "German prophetess" was a title given to Hildegard by her contemporaries. In an illumination that accompanies the text of her visions, she is depicted as being touched by descending tongues of fire as she listens for "the voice from heaven" before writing her text on a wax tablet. Such a medieval image is never just an individual portrait in the modern sense. It rather refers to Hildegard's specific social role as a visionary and prophet who had deep insight into Scripture and could therefore write and speak to the people in the name of God, calling them into an alternative consciousness. This highly unusual "occupation" for a twelfth-century woman was grounded in Hildegard's own conviction, and society's consent, that the visions gave her insight into the deeper meaning of the Christian faith and thus the right to speak to and with authority.

Hildegard's prophetic rather than mystical authority cannot be understood apart from her visionary experience. Similar to the "call visions" of biblical prophets, Hildegard had an overwhelming experience of the reality of the Divine Mystery as the Living Light, which initiated her call to write and speak to the people of God. Like an Old Testament prophet, she situates the exact time and place of the vision, stating that it occurred in the days when Henry was archbishop of Mainz, when Conrad was king of the Romans, when Kuno was abbot of Disibodenberg, and Eugenius was pope:

> It happened in the year 1141 at the Incarnation of the Son of God, Jesus Christ, when I was forty-two years and seven months of age. A fiery light flashed from the open vault of heaven. It permeated my brain and enflamed my heart and the entire breast not like a burning, but like a warming flame, as the sun warms everything its rays touch. And suddenly I was given insight into the meaning of Scripture, namely the Psalter, the Gospel, and the other catholic volumes of both the Old and the New Testaments. But I was not given knowledge of the literal sense of their texts, nor of the division of syllables and the cases or tenses. I have known the power and the mystery of secret and marvelous visions in wonderful ways since my childhood, from my fifth year on, just as I still do today. I revealed this to no one except to a few God-fearing people who were living in the same manner as I. Up to the time, when God through his grace wished it to be revealed, I covered everything with utter silence. The visions which I saw I did not perceive in dreams, or sleep, or delirium, or with bodily eyes and the external human ears, nor in remote places. I received them while I was awake and of a

clear mind, with the eyes and ears of the inner self, in open places, according to the will of God. (SC, declaration)

Purification and Illumination

Hildegard prefaces the description of her prophetic call and mission with a dense passage that speaks about her own preparation to respond to God's call, a necessary part of the transformative journey. She "saw" a light of great splendor and "heard" a voice speaking out of this light. The voice she heard bid her to write "according to the will of Him who knows all, sees all, and orders all in the hiddenness of His mysteries":

> I, the Living Light who illuminates the darkness, have placed the human being — whom I have chosen and miraculously stricken — into great wonders according to my will. They surpass the mysteries the ancient seers were allowed to see in me. I cast this human being down to earth so that she would not rise up in self-importance. The world gave her neither cause for joy, nor for inordinate desires or incentives to be involved with things of this world, for I kept her from stubborn audacity. Fear-filled and timid, she performed her work. Intellect and consciousness were in fetters while her body suffered severe illness. Untroubled joy was a stranger and she felt a constant sense of guilt. For I built a fence around the clefts of her heart so that her spirit would not rise in pride and ambition but would gain fear and sorrow rather than joy and presumption. (SC, declaration)

"The Living Light who illuminates all darkness" illumined the darkness in Hildegard's being that had prevented her from perceiving the presence of the Divine Mystery in all there is, in body and soul, in nature and history, in pain and joy. The well of her psyche had to undergo a God-induced purification that entailed mental, physical, and spiritual suffering until she finally started to write. The purification resulted in a dramatic breakthrough into the deepest realm of her consciousness, where she perceived the entire universe as interrelated, as stamped with the relational quality that is the mystery of the Son. She then, gradually, experienced herself as called, redeemed, and enabled by Jesus Christ to speak, write, confront, and counsel. She experienced herself as possessing an inner clarity and a deep desire that helped her bridge the tension of opposites: God and human, light and darkness, body and spirit, heaven and earth, focused consciousness and diffused consciousness, childlike wonder and awe, compassion and confrontation. Yet only after she lived through this painful transformation from conditioned consciousness into a deeper God-consciousness was she able to gradually respond to the call that would make her a visionary and prophetic authority among her contemporaries. The authority to speak to others about the mysteries of God, to participate in the birth pangs of the new creation, was grounded in an attitude of receptivity that allows the "Living Light" to bring life to blossoming and fruition.

"In the Light of Love, Wisdom Teaches Me"

From childhood on, Hildegard had certain clairvoyant gifts that she describes as "seeing in an extraordinary light." In her biography entitled *Vita*, which was completed by two monks shortly after her death, we find some rare autobiographical passages in which Hildegard herself recounts this gift and interprets it from a mature faith-perspective:

> In the light of Love, Wisdom teaches me and bids me to tell how I was put into these visions. The words I speak are not my own, but true Wisdom speaks them through me and thus to me: O human being, hear these words and speak them not according to yourself but according to me and, thus animated by me, speak of yourself like this: In my first formation, when God woke me through the breath of life in my mother's womb, he impressed this way of seeing on my soul. (DL 71)

We also get some insight into an early awareness of her visionary ability. In the third year of her life she saw such a magnificent light that "her soul shuddered," but being a child she could not speak about it. Up to her fifteenth year she saw many things and even foretold future events. Fearful of reactions, she carefully hid this gift, which was accompanied by illness, fears, embarrassment, and tears. Jutta, however, knew about it and spoke to Volmar. Hildegard kept quiet until the prophetic call vision when she was forty-two, which forced her to reveal what she had seen and heard. It differed from prior visions in its power, scope, and demands.

The fullest and most explicit account of how she "saw" is found in a much-quoted letter of reply to the monk Wibert of Gembloux, who asked her all kind of questions. Did she dictate in Latin or German? Did she remember or forget what she saw? Was the source of her understanding Scripture, instruction, or inspiration? Did she see in dreams, awake, or in ecstasy? What did the strange title of her book *Scivias* mean? In her letter of reply she describes the Light as "crystal-clear," of "immense brilliance," as "nonspatial," and as "beyond measure." Hildegard's desire for God was, however, a precondition for her visions:

> I am always filled with trembling fear, as I do not know for certain of any single capacity in me. Yet I stretch out my hands to God, so that, like a feather that lacks all weight and strength and flies through the wind, I may be borne up to him. And I cannot perfectly know the things that I see as long as I am in service to the body and the invisible soul, for in both human beings are imperfect. (DL 64)

Hildegard stresses that her visions were always concurrent with physical sight and that she did not experience the "unconsciousness" of ecstasy:

> I do not hear them with my outward ears, nor do I perceive them by the thoughts of my own heart or by any combination of my five senses. I hear them in my soul alone while my outward eyes are open. I have thus never fallen prey to ecstasy in the visions, but see them wide awake, by day and at night. (DL 64–65)

"Hearing with the soul" is, as Hildegard indicates, not perception through the physical senses. It refers to perception with the spiritual senses, to an awakening of a new quality of perception. It is an inbreaking of a contemplative awareness that is capable of perceiving all reality as illumined and suffused by God, as graced with tremendous potential. For Hildegard this perception led to bold proclamations of the God-reality to her contemporaries. The awakening of the spiritual senses can, however, happen to all of us. It is not necessarily tied to great visionary gifts. We are all capable of "hearing with the soul."

In her letter to Wibert of Gembloux, Hildegard describes being awake in the Mystery of God in terms of being in the presence of the Living Light. She reveals that there were two modes of vision, one much more intense, rare, and indescribable than the other:

> The brightness that I see is not spatial, yet it is far more lucent than a cloud that envelops the sun. I cannot contemplate height or length or breadth in it; and I call it "the shadow of the living brightness." And as sun, moon, and stars appear [mirrored] in water, so Scripture, discourses, virtues, and some works of men take form for me and are reflected in its brightness.
>
> Whatever I have seen or learned in this vision, I retain the memory of it for a long time,...and I see, hear, and know simultaneously, and learn what I know as if in a moment. But what I do not see I do not know, for I am not learned. And the things I write are those I see and hear through the vision, nor do I set down words other than those I hear; I utter them in unpolished Latin, just as I hear them through the vision....
>
> And in the same brightness I sometimes, not often, see another light, which I call "the Living Light"; when or how I see it, I cannot express; and for the time I do see it, all sadness and all anguish is taken from me, so that then I have tho air of an innocent young girl and not of a little old woman.
>
> Yet because of the constant illness that I suffer, I at times weary of expressing the words and the visions that are shown to me; nonetheless, when my soul, tasting, sees those things, I am transformed to act so differently that, as I said, I consign all pain and affliction to oblivion. And what I see and hear in the vision then, my soul drains as from a fountain — yet the fountain stays full and never drainable. (DR 168–69)

Worried about the implications of her gifts, Hildegard wrote to Bernard of Clairvaux, her famous contemporary:

Father, I am greatly disturbed by a vision which has appeared to me through divine revelation, a vision not seen with my fleshly eyes but only in my spirit. Wretched, and indeed more wretched in my womanly condition, I have from earliest childhood seen great marvels which my tongue has no power to express but which the Spirit of God has taught me that I may believe. Steadfast and gentle father, in your kindness respond to me, your unworthy servant, who has never, from earliest childhood, lived one hour free from anxiety....

I have been placed in your care so that you might reveal to me through our correspondence whether I should speak these things openly or keep my silence, because I have great anxiety about this vision with respect to how much I should speak about what I have seen and heard. In the meantime, because I have kept silent about this vision, I have been laid down, bedridden in my infirmities, and am unable to raise myself up.

...And so I beseech your aid, through the serenity of the Father and through His wondrous Word and through the sweet moisture of compunction, the Spirit of truth (cf. John 14:17; 16:13), and through that holy Sound, which all creation echoes, and through that same Word which gave birth to the world, and through the sublimity of the Father, who sent the Word with sweet fruitfulness into the womb of the Virgin, from which He soaked up flesh, just as honey is surrounded by the honeycomb. And may that Sound, the power of the Father, fall upon your heart and lift up your spirit so that you may respond expeditiously to these words of mine. (L 27–28)

Hildegard assumed that, like herself, Bernard "heard" with the spiritual sense. She spoke of the "holy Sound that all creation echoes" and asked this same Sound to lift up Bernard's heart. Bernard replied:

We rejoice in the grace of God which is in you. And, further, we most earnestly urge and beseech you to recognize this gift of grace and to respond eagerly to it with all humility and devotion, with the knowledge that "God resisteth the proud and giveth grace to the humble" (James 4:1; 1 Pet. 5:5). But, on the other hand, when learning and the anointing (which reveals all things to you) are within, what advice could we possibly give? (L 31)

Soon afterward, in 1148, Bernard spoke in favor of Hildegard at the synod in Trier. Hildegard's writings had been brought to the pope's attention and her visionary gift investigated. Pope Eugenius himself read to the assembled prelates from her book, confirmed her prophetic gift through his authority, and encouraged her to write her visions down. Slowly, painfully, over the span of many years, Hildegard translated her visionary experiences of the Mystery of God into words. She wrote down the visions, then gave a theological interpretation, and finally had illuminations of the visions drawn under her supervision.

Listening to Hildegard with "the Ears of the Heart"

Hildegard's writings are extremely difficult for modern readers. She uses her visionary experiences as "texts" that are then interpreted in the style of her century. Her consciousness and her ways of speaking and interpreting are strange for modern readers. They were historically and culturally conditioned. Hildegard's symbolic images and language, however, strike a resonance within the depths of our psyche and reveal a precious kernel of transcultural meaning. They need refocusing and translation for men and women today who face a complex modern world with a very different mentality and consciousness. In Hildegard we can discover a partner in conversation, a woman who calls us to a contemplative perspective for the building of the human community here on earth. She stands as an example and reminder of the inner movement of Love that stirs in the depths of our being and wants to become incarnate in our actions. This inner stirring calls us to wake up to its presence and to become conscious participants in the interrelated web of life that reveals the mystery of a Trinitarian God. Her theological term for this profound interrelatedness is *viriditas*, a mutuality and fecundity that is the work of Christ and the human task.

It is, however, not easy to gain access to Hildegard's complex, symbolic universe; it is not easy to penetrate and receive her texts, which need translation from one culture to another. In the process of translating her body of thought, I leave some texts behind when I highlight, re-cast, and re-tell others with the intent to build a new house for the old text. Let me show you the three bridges that have helped me cross the abyss of the centuries: (1) Hildegard's choice of symbolic, archetypal language; (2) Benedictine spirituality; and (3) the female experience as filter and lens. Below, I examine each of the bridges, in the hope that my discussion can help lead others across the centuries.

Symbolic, Archetypal Language

One of the ways to break through the historical conditioning of her writings is to focus on the symbolic, archetypal images of her visions. Profound visionary experiences of the Mystery of God seared the core of her psyche. They broke through the frontiers of categories of meaning and opened them to greater depths. She came to know herself and all the world as being deeply loved by God yet caught in patterns of behavior that prevent or oppose this reality. From the core of this awakening she groped for images, metaphors, and archetypal symbols that would somehow point to this reality and reveal an inner map for the landscape where God's Spirit and the human spirit meet. Words and images rose from the depth of her being to communicate the reality of God's mystery experienced by her. They resonated with the words and images from Scripture and tradition that spoke to her deep identity and ordered her days, yet her own language goes beyond them. As symbols, they have the power to resonate with our own spiritual sensitivity. The topography of the realm of the Spirit that Hildegard describes had already been charted by her tradition. She expands our knowledge of this rich landscape by adding to this symbolic map the realms where God's Spirit and our spirit meet and produce fecundity — the realms of *viriditas*, or greening power.

Hildegard weaves the images and archetypal symbols that point to this territory into two great mythic stories about God: God's presence throughout history and God's presence as revealed in the entire cosmos. Interweaving these two stories, she broadens the base of how we understand who we are, of how God desires to become more fully present in all of reality.

This is Hildegard's specific way of doing theology, of speaking clearly but not systematically about God. She draws on the wisdom and stories of our identity as a people of God, and at the same time she draws on the wisdom of nature, of the universe. Living her life on the wings of faith and shaped by a tradition, Hildegard added a focus on wholeness, on integrity, on interconnectedness. All of life is meant to be interrelated, she tells us: "Everything exists to respond to the other." The macrocosm of the universe and the microcosm of the human being, body and psyche, are both energized by *viriditas,* the fecundity that has its source in God and in our response to God. Using biblical images and archetypal symbols that she found "more suited for divine things than the naked word," Hildegard interweaves the story of God's presence in history with the story of God's presence in the cosmos and asks us to live lives that reveal and embody this presence. She creates a precious mosaic, a parable of the fullness of life and its counterforces. One of her powerful images is that of the entire cosmos and the human at its center as embraced by the fiery circle of the Cosmic Christ, as resting in the womb or heart of God.

Great mythic stories are not concerned with factual accuracy or morality. They reveal a truth that is universal; they tell us something about our identity, about who we are and what we are supposed to become. The biblical images and archetypal symbols of the great parable Hildegard tells can provide a map for our personal and communal journey. They call us into sacred spaces of awareness where true partnership with the earth and all its inhabitants becomes possible, where our involvement with life loses a self-centered focus, where we become aware of the transcendent and liberating Mystery of God.

Symbolic imagery is the primary language of our psyche, as Carl Jung, a modern explorer of the psyche, points out. In our age we generally have lost the ability to hear this language in anything but poetry, art, or other efforts we judge to be creative. This is a real impoverishment, for the psyche of every person has the potential both to create and to hear this symbolic language that can compensate for a one-sided or restricted perception of reality. Archetypal images became the "language" for Hildegard's visionary experience of the Mystery of God and for the two great mythic stories she interweaves.

These images evoke rather than explain and can resonate with our own hearts. In her visions Hildegard experienced the life-giving, ever-present energy of God that opened the meaning of the Scriptures for her and asked her to speak and write. It is almost impossible to fit such an experience into known categories of language or thought. Like writers of the Hebrew Scriptures or the Gospels, she uses poetic, symbolic language as a means to communicate the ineffable reality of her experiences. Her archetypal images and prophetic words create bridges between her experiences and our deepest longings, between the cosmic, divine order and the depth of the human psyche. They create bridges between our personal story and the story of the human community, bridges between human beings in historical settings and human beings as one part of the great web of nature. Many of her visionary images are in mandala form. Mandalas function as patterns of order, as centering symbols that allow the confusion of the individual psyche to become part of a larger order.

Like an ancient seer or a prophet of the Old Testament, Hildegard calls her contemporaries and us to wake up to the Mystery of God in all there is, and was, and ever will be. If this is a true awakening from God-forgetfulness (*oblivio Dei*) and not just an intellectual consent, it will result in spiritual tasks that break out of all confines of a narrow understanding of spirituality. It will be an awakening to our wounds and to our potential to become co-creators with God. It will be an awakening to our need for God's grace. For whatever human beings do impacts both history and nature, Hildegard tells us. Good works, the *opus bonum*, are both task and gift. They become possible when true discernment of good and evil has been threaded through the narrow gate of good works. They become possible when true repentance, which has its roots in the Passion of the incarnate Son, is transformed into world-renewing energies.

Benedictine Spirituality

Another way to approach Hildegard's difficult writings is to look at her as a Benedictine nun. She was a woman of deep faith, an abbess, whose life was ordered by the Rule of St. Benedict and immersed in the great biblical stories of God's relationship with us in creation and history. Since her early childhood her days had been punctuated by eight periods of prayer, the chanting of the Divine Office. Hildegard's identity was shaped by the Bible and probably touched by the emotional honesty of the Psalms she recited daily. It was shaped and nourished by the texts of Scripture, by the concreteness and vitality of the Rule of St. Benedict, by life in community, and, last but not least, by her own response to her visionary gifts. The Benedictine spirituality she lived calls for listening, balance, focus, and ongoing conversion until one's life itself becomes a sacred poem. "Seeking God," the end all of Benedictine life, is nourished by the savoring of Scripture, that *lectio divina* whose aim is wisdom, contemplation, and desire, not knowledge in the modern sense. In monastic culture Scripture alone reveals the criteria for living life well — circumstances in real life are its testing ground where the crossroads of decision are reached. On our own modern journey from the head to the heart the wisdom of Benedictine life can be of great help.

Listen, the Rule of St. Benedict advises, listen with the "ears of your heart." Listening with the ears of the heart refers to a type of contemplative listening, an experiential awareness of the Divine Mystery in the circumstances of life. This kind of consciousness, of tasted intimacy with God, which like prayer arises from the depth of one's being, is beyond explanation. It can only be described by analogy to physical sense experience. Tradition, since Origin in the third century, has referred to this contemplative consciousness as the "spiritual senses." Just as we have five physical senses, so we have five spiritual senses, some of which can be awakened at a certain stage of the spiritual journey. Expressions like "hearing God," "seeing God," being "embraced by God," and even "tasting God" are poetic renderings that point to the perception of these senses. When the Rule of St. Benedict advises a listening with "the ears of the heart," it refers to the consciousness spoken of as a spiritual sense. This kind of savoring of the love of God was taught in Hildegard's monastic formation. It is, however, the birthright of all God's children, a potential that needs focus and practice. We are all capable of "opening our eyes to the light that comes from God," as the prologue to the Rule advises:

"It is high time for us to arise from sleep" (Rom. 13:11). Let us open our eyes to the light that comes from God, and our ears to the voice from heaven that every day calls out this charge: "If you hear God's voice today, do not harden your hearts" (Ps. 94[95]:8). And again: "You that have ears to hear, listen to what the Spirit says to the churches" (Rev. 2:7). And what does the Spirit say? "Come and listen to me and I will teach you the fear of the Lord" (Ps. 33[34]:12). "Run while you have the light of life, that the darkness of death may not overtake you" (John 12:35). (RB, prologue 8–13)

This kind of listening and seeing with an open and contrite heart, a listening for the voice of God, a listening for Wisdom's presence in Scripture and in the marketplace, is the theme that runs through all of Hildegard's writings. Hildegard called her contemporaries and us to listen with the "ears of the heart" to the hidden light and sound of God's presence among us. In monastic culture, Scripture was seen as the light that awakens and the sound that rouses. It was interpreted on four levels of images: the literal, the moral, the allegorical, and the anagogical. This kind of perception and interpretation is neither an escape into otherworldly dimensions nor a hiding in rules and doctrine. Hildegard tells us that it will focus our seeking of God and reveal the way. Her writings are deeply rooted in the Benedictine spirituality of choosing the "right way," the way of God, and are filled with references to the contemplative perception referred to as the spiritual senses. "Let us set out on this way with the Gospel as our guide" is how St. Benedict phrased it (RB, prologue 9).

Hildegard described this contemplative focus for us. In a comment on a quote from the Book of Revelation (21:10–11), she speaks about seeing "with eyes that see the inner things" and then gives some insight on what happens when this spiritual sense is opened:

The Spirit lifts the spirit. How? The Holy Spirit in its power draws the human spirit out of the burden of the flesh so that it may fly in the vision of those eyes that see the inner things.... What does this mean? The Holy Spirit lifts the human spirit up to the mountain of heavenly desires so that it may clearly see which works need to be done, need to be accomplished in the Spirit of God. (SC III, 10, 31)

Hildegard wrote her first book, *Scivias* (Know the Ways of God), after her powerful prophetic call vision commanded her to speak and write. To put her ineffable visionary experiences into adequate words, images, and interpretations took ten years. Her writings resound with biblical allusions. Each vision ends with a stern admonition to listen to the words that were revealed by the Living Light, to listen with the spiritual senses. The admonitions differ for each of the three sections of the book and show a progression in God-awareness that enables a perception of the Real with a new and deepened sensitivity of body and soul, with the spiritual senses:

Whoever has knowledge in the Holy Spirit and wings of faith, should not ignore my admonition, but taste them and embrace with their soul. (SC I, 1–6)

Whoever sees this with watchful eyes and hears with resounding ears should kiss and embrace the mysterious words which flow from Me, the Living One. (SC II, 1–7)

Whoever has sharpened ears of inner discernment should pant for these words in ardent love for My Reflection and inscribe them in the conscience of the soul. (SC III, 1–13)

If we want to fruitfully enter Hildegard's powerful, holistic worldview, if we desire the interrelatedness of the web of life that reveals the Mystery of God she speaks about, then we have to find modern ways to relate to the opening of those spiritual senses. We might have to ground ourselves in the Benedictine spiritual roots Hildegard represents. We have to find contemporary ways to holiness, ways that are not confined to life in the cloister, ways that let us seek God right in the depth of everyday life, right in the depth of creation and history, and right in the depth of Scripture. The Mystery of God can be experienced as the life force (*viriditas*) that shapes, nourishes, and confronts our seeking of God in all of life, Hildegard assures us.

The Female Experience as Filter and Lens
Modern scholarship points out that all experience is gendered, is shaped by the cultural experience of being male and female

as well as by the particular consciousness of living in a male or female body. In her visions, Hildegard not only experienced the challenge to become a prophet and to speak in God's name; she also experienced a profound affirmation of herself as a woman. An amazing sentence is revealing:

> Praise, therefore, praise God, you blessed hearts, for all the miracles God has wrought in the female presentation of beauty of the Most High, which He Himself foresaw when she appeared, for the first time, in the rib of man whom God had created. (SC III, 13, 16)

Although Hildegard describes herself as a poor, unlearned woman, she was able to forge a theology of wisdom, of the fertility she calls *viriditas*, which desires embodiment. She was unlearned in comparison with men of her age, yet her experiences of the Living Light called her into a confidence and authority that go way beyond the conditioning and consciousness of her culture. As a woman graced by God and called to speak out, Hildegard gives us new and very feminine images of the God-reality, like the visionary image of "the cosmos resting in the womb of God." This specific image is not found in the theological or biblical tradition.

The visionary experience of God's self-disclosure in the depth of her being needed expression in words and images that would ring most true with her being as a woman. As we shall see later, it is likely that Hildegard's experience of the deep affirmation of her own womanhood by God was what enabled her to break the shackles of conditioned perception. It was for Hildegard to recognize and name the fecundity of God that wants to become incarnate in history. The unusual term for this fecundity, *viriditas*, arose from the depth of this woman when her experience of the divine desire was filtered through her female experience and imagination. It is a word that uses a woman's ability to bear life in the womb of her being as a metaphor for God's presence in the womb of all of life. For human beings, however, this potential for a fecundity of interrelatedness does entail a willingness to groan in labor pains while bringing the Kingdom-reality to birth.

Modern scholarship points out that men and women have different styles of consciousness. In contrast to a masculine style of consciousness, which strives for clear focus and a specific, detached observance, the feminine style of consciousness moves toward completeness and relationship, whether it be with a person, an idea, or a historical event. This connected kind of knowing emerges strongly as Hildegard comes to fuller consciousness through the acceptance of God's call and her willingness to wrestle with the unknown territory between received God-images and God's self-disclosure to her. Hildegard's term *viriditas* rose from a deeply innate mode of being a woman who was willing to live in that unknown territory. As a woman she speaks of God. She does theology not as abstract thinking but as a laboring to give birth to the Mystery in history. Her image of the cosmos resting in the womb of God was forged in the depth of her feminine psyche. It was slowly and reluctantly embraced, harnessed for others, and thus made creative and fruitful. Her "gendered" experience shaped her symbolic theology of history in a specific way. It enabled her to focus on "the birthing of interrelatedness in cosmos and history" as the work of the incarnate Word and our task.

Her words and images about the Divine Mystery, her theology, arose from a contemplative center in dialogue with Scripture and tradition, not from learned scholastic debate. Her visionary experiences changed not only her self-perception and her God-image but also the way in which she could perceive the depth dimension of events and people she met. She perceived all of reality as laboring to give birth to an unbroken web of all living things. In my view, this depth perception has a specific coloration because it is filtered through her female experience. Her social context and conditioning were the primary lenses through which reality and identity were filtered. The depth dimension was added when she finally consented to speak from the affirmation and challenge of her visionary experiences about the mystery that is the hidden power in all events, in all ages, in all of nature.

The notion of fecundity, *viriditas*, tells us something about the mothering nature of God, in whose image and likeness we are made. But it also tells us something about ourselves, men and women who are made in the image of God. In our age the feminine mode of personally receiving, embodying, and relating to the mystery of our God can become the dark womb-tent where Wisdom is waiting to be born into the world.

The three bridges I explored can lead us, like Hildegard, into the territory of fecundity where God's grace and human response meet. If we become pregnant with God's grace, we usually learn to gradually "house" all of ourselves, the good and the bad, the fears and the potentials, the conditioned and the free parts, the idols and the deep longings. Only then — with others, and in the shelter of God's Love — do we become capable of "housing" the full impact of the world's sorrow, as well as the pulsations of the Living Light in all of reality, that demand our response.

Chapter 3

The Living Light

Hildegard's life was burdened and changed by visions of God as the Living Light. Her prophetic and imaginative response to the visions was rooted in the Gospel and the needs of her time. Hildegard tells us that she found poetic, symbolic language "more suitable for teaching divine things than the naked word." Symbols speak a universal language as they strike the heart and captivate the mind. They can point toward the glory and challenge of God's elusive yet irresistible presence and root personal experience in that of the greater community.

Symbolic thinking is one way in which some splits we have inherited can be healed: the split between the head and the heart, between theology and spirituality. Hildegard once said that if people pick up more knowledge with the head than their hearts can digest, they become ill. Don't we modern people often move from intellectual insight into activism without digesting either acquired knowledge or the resulting actions in the cave of the heart? Without the pollinating presence of healed or healing emotions, our actions cannot bear fruit, Hildegard tells us. On an experiential level, our ideas about God often undergo a transformation in the crucible of broken symbols and ideas, while new ones are molded on the foundation of our God-experiences.

In the following chapters we will look at some key symbols in Hildegard's visionary framework. They provide precious, multicolored windows into the graced reality Hildegard speaks about: hearts transformed in Christ and the earth, sanctified by human choice, becoming God's dwelling place. Hildegard unites symbols of conflicting realities into the hidden heartbeat of God: the Living Light and the aridity of sin; the Mystery of God and a world imprisoned in fear; the cosmos resting in the womb and eternal embrace of God and our earth crying out as it is becoming a wasteland.

Here in chapter 3 the focus is on the Living Light and on *viriditas*, the "work of the Word," as symbols that emerged from the depths of Hildegard's God-experience. Chapter 4 looks at what Hildegard tells us about living in a cosmos where everything that exists is meant to respond to the other. Hildegard's powerful symbol for this reality is the cosmos — with the human being in its center — as a living organ in the womb of God. Chapter 5 focuses on Hildegard's symbols for the union of body and soul and for the partnership of man and woman. Chapter 6 describes the "way of the heart," while chapter 7 explores Hildegard's depiction of a life lived "in the tension of opposites," a depiction that abounds with symbolic representations of attitudes that reside in the human heart. Chapter 8 introduces a wide array of symbolic representations of *Discretio* — discernment that is needed when we stand at "the crossroads of decision." That chapter also looks at Divine Wisdom — who builds her house in history and in the "Heavenly Jerusalem" — as a symbol for faith and hope for our communal journey to build the Kingdom. For this journey we need *rationalitas*, bright-burning understanding, an ability gained when we seek the God who is Love in all we do. Chapter 9 looks at Love (*Caritas*) as the matrix for creation, redemption, and the bright-burning understanding that is both gift and task for human beings. Hildegard's unusual image of the Trinity, the final symbol we look at, points to a deep theological truth and also to the human ability to become — in and through the grace of Christ — the earth for the dynamic fecundity of the Trinitarian Love.

All of Hildegard's symbols point to a reality that is not yet fully present here and now, a reality that calls into question the way things are. Whenever we read Hildegard's symbolic language as a mere description of her own experiences, its symbolic power to call us into creative fecundity and interrelatedness is lost. That is, we must let her symbols be a guide to the reality of God in all of life and to the fires of our own experience.

Hildegard's book *Scivias* is a fireworks of brilliant visionary images, many in mandala form, that point the reader toward

God's ways, which should also be our ways. According to Hildegard, the Mystery of God reveals one great pattern. All of creation, including the matter of the universe, emerged from God's Love (*Caritas*) and has Christ, the Wisdom of God, as its manifestation, goal, and explanation. The entire universe is meant to reveal the interrelational, Trinitarian energy pattern of Love. Human beings are meant to participate in this pattern of fecundity (*viriditas*), which is the work of the Son (*Opus autem Verbi viriditas est* [the work of the Word is fecundity]) (CC I, 22, 15).

In a letter to Abbot Adam, Hildegard speaks about Divine Love this way: "She has her dwelling place in eternity. For when God wished to create the world, he bent down in sweetest love, and He provided for all necessary things, just as a father prepares the inheritance for his son. Thus it was in great ardor that He established all His works in order" (L 193).

In the first vision of *Scivias,* her prophetic call vision (see illumination 1), we can already discern this pattern. It becomes more explicit and specific in later writings:

> I saw something like a great iron-colored mountain. Enthroned on it was a figure of such brilliance that his glory blinded my sight. On each side of him, like wings of wondrous breadth and length, a soft shadow extended. Before him, at the foot of the mountain, stood a figure covered all over with eyes. Because of all those eyes, I could not even discern a human shape. In front of this figure stood another one, a child wearing a pale tunic and white shoes. On its head descended such brightness from the One who sat on the mountain, that I could not see her face. From the One who sat enthroned upon the mountain, many living sparks sprang forth, which surrounded the figures with a delightful glow. In the mountain itself I saw many little windows in which human heads appeared, some pale and some white. (SC I,1)

She sees a Christ figure enthroned on a mountain that symbolizes the Kingdom of God, enfolding it with wings of "boundless justice, which persevered in a true balance of just and loving protection." The mountain is an age-old symbol for encounters with God's elusive presence (Moses, the

Illumination 1
Prophetic Call Vision

Transfiguration, the Sermon on the Mount). The figure is of such fiery glory that it blinds her sight. Christ, God's light and presence, protects the dark womb of the earth like a mother hen.

Like the seer of Patmos at his vision of the Apocalypse, or St. Paul on the road to Damascus, Hildegard is overwhelmed by the visionary experience of perceiving the Mystery of God as the source of all there is. One might expect to see an image of Hildegard herself in this vision, but instead we meet only the "Fear of the Lord" as the primary attitude for encountering the God-reality. This archetypal figure — so fully awake and filled with desire for God that her whole being becomes eyes — represents the biblical attitude of reverence and awe. The archetypal image of the figure who is "all eyes" is strikingly original, yet it resonates with the Rule of St. Benedict, where "Fear of the Lord" is the first step on the ladder of humility. "Let us open our eyes to the light that comes from God," Benedict advises. Being awake is understood as being totally focused in awe on the Mystery of God — Hildegard's response to the visionary revelation of the fiery Christ. It is an attitude she asks us to take. A stream of brilliant light flows from the book on Christ's lap and totally engulfs the head of the girl child, "Poverty of Spirit," which inevitably follows the "Fear of the Lord," as Hildegard tells us. Walking in the traces of the Son of God, "Poverty of Spirit" attributes all her just works to God alone. Ribbons of living sparks surround both figures. They symbolize the creative powers of God's Love that were lived and set free in Jesus, the Christ. According to Hildegard, these creative powers of God protect and aid those humans who live in fear of the Lord and in poverty of spirit; they become manifestations of divine-human synergy. The iron-colored mountain symbolizes the stability and indestructibility of the Kingdom and also the labor pains of bringing this reality about. In the womblike mountain of the Kingdom there is a multitude of windows, each of which shows two people. This is a visionary image of the "two ways" or two motivations that are present in the human heart: "Sometimes they slumber in weariness of heart and action; sometimes they awake and keep an honoring watch" (SC I, 1, 5). Hildegard, throughout her writings, will symbolize the progressive building of the Kingdom-reality as the "Heavenly Jerusalem." As later chapters will show, Hildegard uses this scriptural theme to point to the depth dimension of reality on earth rather than to an otherworldly reality.

The symbols in the call vision give a holographic image of what Hildegard experienced in the Living Light as God's intent and as the human potential to receive and manifest it. The visionary experience is diffused into a rainbow of biblical allusions and a wide spectrum of meanings that point to the interdependence of God, human beings, and the entire cosmos. Christ, the eternal Word, the "Dawn of Justice," is imaged as the historical Jesus (indicated by the Gospel book) who has become the Christ of faith. As the Cosmic Christ, he is the manifestation and power of "the Living Light," Hildegard's term for the Mystery of God. The Son of Man, who came to serve, now enfolds the Kingdom in wings of divine justice with the yearning, life-giving, discerning sorrow of a mother bird (the image Jesus used for himself in his lament over Jerusalem). Christ, God's Wisdom, is depicted winged like the Sophia icons in the Eastern churches. The desire "to take shelter in the refuge of your wings" (Psalm 61) and the ways to live this out are indicated by the two personified attitudes that can lead human beings toward that full receptivity and fecundity that were fully achieved in Mary and restored to us in the Paschal Mystery.

Hildegard wrote many hymns of praise for Mary that highlight the receptivity that made the Incarnation possible. Mary represents the full expression of that same receptivity that Hildegard advises in the first vision of *Scivias*:

> Resplendent jewel and unclouded brightness
> of the sunlight streaming through you,
> know that the sun is a fountain leaping
> from the father's heart,
> his all-fashioning word.
> He spoke and the primal matrix
> teemed with things unnumbered—
> but Eve unsettled them all.
>
> To you the father spoke again
> but this time

the word he uttered was a man
in your body.
Matrix of light! through you he breathed forth
all that is good,
as in the primal matrix he formed
all that has life. (SY 115)

Christ, the Wisdom of God

When she was sixty-five years old, Hildegard had another overwhelming visionary experience of the Living Light. It was so
profound and overpowering that her body broke down in illness when the heavenly voice told her: "Write down what I
tell you." It took her seven years to write *De operatione Dei*
(The Book of Divine Works), her cosmological book that shows
the intimate connection between the world, human beings, and
God. Twenty-three years of contending with words and images
to reveal something of the mystery she experienced separate
this book from her first one. Her God-image has sharpened;
her theology is becoming a cosmology. The Love of God, which
she experienced as the Living Light, now becomes explicit as
the incarnate Word of God. The Word was always present in
the eternal counsel of God and revealed its mysterious fool-
ishness and fecundity in the Incarnation and Passion of Jesus,
the Christ. Hildegard tells us that the transforming powers of
his life, death, and resurrection are now at work in the entire
universe. The Word became man in order to bring human beings and all of creation to the fullness of creation. This fiery
Trinitarian love of God inflames the very depth of the human
psyche, encouraging discernment of the right way so that together Christ and the human can give birth to actions of Love,
to manifestations of *viriditas*.

In the first vision of *De Operatione Dei*, entitled "About the
Origin of Life" (see illumination 2), Hildegard "sees" the Love
of God (*Caritas*) as a magnificent winged figure whose face
is ablaze with beauty and clarity. An older face appears in a
golden circle above her head. Love carries a lamb, marked with
the cross as the sign of victory, in her arms. With her feet she
treads upon a monster, her two sets of wings encircle the entire
cosmos:

Illumination 2
The Eternally Alive One

The figure spoke this way:

"I, the highest and fiery power, have kindled every living spark and I have breathed out nothing that can die. But I determine how things are — I have regulated the circuit of the heavens by flying around its revolving track with my upper wings — that is to say, with Wisdom. But I am also the fiery light of divine essence — I flame above the beauty of the fields; I shine in the waters; in the sun, the moon, and the stars, I burn. And by means of the airy wind, I stir everything into quickness with a certain invisible life which sustains all. For the air lives in its green power and its blossoming; the waters flow as if they were alive. Even the sun is alive in its own light; and when the waning moon is on the point of disappearing, it is kindled by the sun, so that it lives, as it were, afresh. I have also set up the pillars that sustain the orb of the earth, as well as those winds which have subordinate wings (that is to say, gentler winds) which, through their mildness, hold the stronger winds in check, so that they do not prove a danger. In the same way, the body covers and encloses the soul so that it does not rush out.

For just as the breathing of the soul holds the body together by supporting it, so that it does not fail, so too the strong winds animate the subordinate winds so that they function as they should. And so I, the fiery power, lie hidden in these things and they blaze from me, just as man is continually moved by his breath, and as the fire contains the nimble flame. All these things live in their own essence and are without death, since I am Life. I am also rationality, having the wind of the resounding Word (through which all creation was made) and I have breathed into all these things, so that there is nothing mortal in their natures, because I am Life itself. For I am the whole of life — life was not torn from stones; it did not bud from branches; nor is it rooted in the generative power of the male. Rather every living thing is rooted in me. For rationality is the root, but the resounding Word flowers in it.

Hence, because God is rational, how could he not be at work, since all his work blossoms in man he made in his own image and likeness and in whom he expressed all creation according to fixed measure. For it was always the case throughout eternity that God wanted his work, man, to come into being. And when he finished the task, he gave man all the creatures so that he might work with them, just as God had made man as his own work.

But I am also of service since all living things take their radiance from me; and I am the life which remains the same through eternity, having neither beginning nor end; and the same life, working and moving itself is God and yet this life is one in three powers. And so eternity is called the Father, the Word is called the Son and the breath that connects these two is called the Holy Spirit; just as God marked it in man in whom there are body, soul, and rationality.

But the fact that I flame above the beauty of the fields signifies the earth, which is the stuff from which God made man. And my shining in the waters accords with the soul; because just as the water pours over the whole earth, so the soul pervades the whole body. That I glow in the sun and the moon signifies rationality; but the stars are the countless words of rationality. And the fact that by means of the airy wind I stir everything into quickness with a certain invisible life which sustains all, signifies this: those things which advance in growth are animated and sustained by the air and wind and remain quite unchanged in their essence." (DW I, 2)

And again I heard the voice from heaven speaking to me: "God, who created all there is, formed the human according to God's image and likeness.... God so loved them that he destined the human for the place out of which the fallen angel was banned, assigning the human all glory and honor the former had lost along with his everlasting bliss. This is signified in the face you see.

What you perceive — in the Mystery of God...as a magnificent figure built like a human being — signifies the Love of the heavenly Father. It is Love — in the power of the eternal divinity, of exquisite beauty, magnificent in her powers of secret depth! The figure appears in human likeness, because the Son of God redeemed the fallen human being in the service of Love when he clothed himself with flesh. Therefore this face shines with such beauty and clarity that it would be easier to look into the sun than into this face. For the abundance of Love shines and sparkles with such sublime brilliance of gifts that it surpasses human understanding.... It is shown in symbolic form so that we might know with the eyes of faith what can't be seen with the outer eyes." (WM I, 3)

Only faith, in an attitude of profound awe, can fathom the abundance of this Love which surpasses all understanding: that God redeemed human beings through the Incarnation of his Son and strengthened them through the outpouring of the Holy Spirit.... In the whole work and eternal counsel of God this was the summit of Divine Love: The Son of God, in his humanity, was meant to lead fallen humanity home to the realm of God. (WM I, 4)

What does Hildegard report from the far region where God's Spirit and the human spirit meet? She tells us that she experienced the Mystery of God as a "fiery, ever-living Light of Love." This is something new. "Eternal light" is a term she would have been familiar with through liturgy and the tradition. Visionary light manifestations are found in the Prophets, in the Wisdom Literature, in the texts of St. John and St. Paul, and in the Transfiguration account in Matthew's Gospel. Experiences spoken about as "fire" are found in the Old Testament theophanies, in the description of the descent of the Holy Spirit at Pentecost, and in the image of the Son of Man "who has eyes like a burning flame" (Rev. 1:14). Even Jesus refers to fire in his enigmatic saying that points to the Paschal Mystery: "I have come to bring fire to earth, and how I wish it were blazing already" (Luke 12:49). "Fiery, ever-living Light of Love" is Hildegard's alone.

Hildegard experienced this fire of Christ's Love, Wisdom incarnate, as blazing in nature and history, as ever-living and enkindling all that is frozen and not in relationship with God or this world. Her experience finds its expression not in abstract concepts but in symbolic language that points toward this mystery and invites our participation. The archetypal images of her symbolic theology resonate like poetry with the depth of the human heart, which desires the Holy and needs to ponder Wisdom. They also reveal the universal story of which we are all part. The entire universe, the cosmos, manifests the mystery of this fiery, ever-living Light of Love that shines forth in and through matter, in and through human beings in their specific historical setting. God, as the mystery of Love, is like the horizon that surrounds the human spirit, wooing it into creative tension between body and soul, mind and emotion, individual and community, heaven and earth. Willingness to live in the tension of these poles is the womb that nourishes and protects those discerning actions that will mirror the fiery, life-giving Love that is God. The elimination of evil and unrelatedness in all its forms results from God's initiative and human cooperation:

> O slow people, why do you not come? Would not help be given you, if you sought to come? When you begin to go in God's ways, gnats and flies buzz and hinder you; but take up the fan of the inspiration of the Holy Spirit, and drive them away as fast as possible. You should run, and you should hope for God's help. (SC III, 9, 1)

The inmost power of God's Love, which Hildegard calls the Zeal or Fervor of God (*Zelus Dei*), is always the initiating partner. She depicts this Zeal as a fiery red head that has a terrifying human face turned in anger toward the north, the realm of evil and unconnectedness. Three wings "of wondrous breadth and length, white like a cloud," extend from the head, beating fiercely from time to time. The Zeal of God is always present, but it is experienced in different ways. When human beings are getting in touch with the source of their being, when they are truly seeking God, then the Zeal of God will be experienced as light, fascination, and connectedness. The experience is like an act of conception in that deep inner space of the heart where good and evil are discerned, where *viriditas* becomes possible. The inmost power of God's Love desires to live in and among us in this world. When, however, human beings live with hardened hearts in the exile of God-forgetfulness and ego-centeredness, then they experience the Zeal of God as a consuming firestorm, as a two-edged sword, or as a torturous demand, until they turn to God with tears of repentance. Repentance is the world-renewing power that enables us to become co-workers of God in and for this world, Hildegard tells us. The fiery power of God's Love is always waiting, judging, beating back the powers of evil, with our help:

> Therefore let each person perform works of justice in the joy of the Holy Spirit, and not hesitate and perversely murmur; let him not say that he lacks anything, when he has the first root placed in him by God's gift and the fiery grace of the Holy Spirit, which touches that root by admonition. For if he were thus to fall into perversity, his reprehensible urge would bring him into anguish; his interior root would be diminished, and he would fall farther into compulsion. And then he would truly murmur to himself, "alas, alas! what have I done, not being able to discern my works in God?" So let him also go forward without the burden of unbelief; let him not distrust God in his works, but avoid evil deeds and thus be safe from tearful lamentation.
>
> But let the one who has ears sharp to hear inner meanings ardently love My reflection and pant after My Words, and inscribe them in his soul and conscience. (SC III, 5, 33)

Hildegard does not explain who God is. She rather expresses her experience of God's action and all-pervading presence in symbolic images and analogies of embodiment. Filtered through the female experience, the mystery is spoken of in different, yet very traditional, terms: the Incarnation was the summit of Divine Love, the embodiment of God through which humanity was redeemed (WM I, 4). Body, soul, and emotions are the places where consent to live in the creative tension of opposites becomes the womb for God's presence in the pattern of Mary's consent. In one of the Sequences to the Virgin, Hildegard with great boldness praises the mystery of the conception of the Savior:

> Strong rib of Adam! Out of you
> God sculpted woman: the mirror
> of all his charms, the caress
> of his whole creation. So voices
>
> chime in heaven and the whole
> earth marvels at Mary,
> beloved beyond measure....

Cry, cry aloud! A serpent
hissed and a sea of grief
seeped through his forked
words into the woman. The mother

of us all miscarried.
With ignorant hands she
plucked at her womb and bore
woe without bound.

But the sunrise from your thighs
burnt the whole of her guilt away.
More than all that Eve lost
is the blessing you won.

Mary, savior,
mother of light:
may the limbs of your son be the chords of the song
the angels chant above. (SY 129–31)

Do the symbolic images examined in this chapter resonate with something in your own God-experience? If they do, then they also tell you something about your own spiritual journey. Our personal journey, however, is part of a much larger spiritual journey in the creative/redemptive pattern Hildegard describes so well. Hildegard shifts our focus from "my love for God" to "God's Love for us." God's Love for us, which is manifested in all of reality, came to full expression in the Incarnation. Explaining that the "ways of the Lord" became visible in the "humanity of the Word of God," Hildegard says:

In place of a covenant God planted the great splendor of the reddish light. He sent His Word filled with desire into it. Without separating from it, He gave it as productive fruit and brought it forth as a great fountain, so that every believer who tasted of it from now on would not die of thirst.... In the brilliance of the reddish light the fecundity [*viriditas*] of the great ancient counsel became manifest. (SC II, 1, 11)

Hildegard does not let us forget that the Word, which became incarnate in time as Jesus (the exemplar of God and of human potential), freely embraced the redemptive Passion (the reddish light). The wholeness of life on earth is regained in that foolish and incomprehensible cruciform pattern of fecundity that speaks of God's Love for us. This pattern takes a multitude of personal shapes and corporate shapes as — in the power of the Resurrection — Divine Wisdom builds her tent in history. For "through the fountain-fullness of the Word came the embrace of God's *maternal* love, which nourishes us into life, is our help in perils, and — as a most profound and gentle love — opens us for repentance" (SC II, 2, 4).

If something in Hildegard's words about God — her theology — rings true for a reader, then this shift in focus might lead to an awareness of God's Love, rather than intellectual knowledge about it. It might lead to growth in receptivity and awe as the primary attitudes needed for the pattern of divine fecundity (*viriditas*) to become embodied in and through human beings in this world. We can become part of the great cosmic process as we treasure and nourish this developing life in the womb of our being and finally endure the labor pains — often experienced as something like a crucifixion — of transforming the fire of Divine Love into tangible historical reality that manifests God. We are "the earth" for God's becoming. An antiphon to the Holy Spirit speaks to this becoming:

> The Spirit of God
> is a life that bestows life,
> root of the world tree
> and wind in its boughs.
>
> Scrubbing out sins,
> she rubs oil into wounds.
>
> She is glistening life
> alluring all praise,
> all-awakening,
> all-resurrecting. (SY 141)

The Work of the Word Is Fecundity
(*Opus autem verbi viriditas est*)

Hildegard speaks about her visionary revelations of the Divine Mystery from her faith-experience as a woman. Caroline Walker Bynum has pointed out that experience is always "gendered" and that symbolic expressions may mean something different for women and men. How Hildegard charts the "way of God" is influenced by the fact that she is a woman theologian.

In *Sister of Wisdom: St. Hildegard's Theology of the Feminine*, Barbara Newman situates Hildegard in the "sapiential tradition," the strand of Christian thought that focuses on the presence of Divine Wisdom in creation and redemption. She illustrates how Hildegard's many symbolic images of Wisdom and of Love represent the feminine aspect of God and how Hildegard explores the meaning of being a woman within the divine plan.

Hildegard's original term, *viriditas* (fecundity), very likely arises from the same sapiential thread. The profound affirmation of being a woman before God opened that free creative space in which new consciousness can emerge. Hildegard expanded woman's capacity to nourish new life in her womb into the great all-embracing depth of a theological truth that we came from the heart of God and that the earth is the womb of our becoming whole, for and with each other in God. The female experience as filter and lens has given us a term that talks as much about God as it refers to creation/redemption and the capacity of all humans, both men and women, to nourish new life in the womb of history, to become co-creators with God. Hildegard saw redemption as the birthing of interrelatedness in history and cosmos, as the work of Christ in which we participate. The up-building of the Kingdom in history is informed and transformed by *viriditas* in the pattern and power of Christ, the Wisdom of God.

Love/Wisdom/*viriditas* shone forth in the Son of God who became man. We human beings can — through grace — participate in the power of these divine energies (*virtutes*) he set free and experience them like the loving maternal care of God. In her commentary on the Prologue to the Gospel of John, Hildegard puts it this way:

> "*Any who did accept him he empowered to become children of God.*" Human beings of both genders, who accepted Him in faith as God and man (for God is first known by faith, only then as man), received from His abundant strength the power of free decision to become children of God in the

heavenly Kingdom. This means that as heirs of His legacy they participate with Him in His Kingdom, indeed in the same strength out of which the Son is the heir of His Father. They who accepted Him as their God and creator, who embraced Him in love, and gave Him the kiss of faith, who let Him explore the depth of their being eagerly and carefully, all these were inundated by the dew of the Holy Spirit. Out of them the church began to sprout and to bear fruit of profound joy. (WM IV, 179-80)

Another time "the voice from heaven" admonished Hildegard to "Speak openly about the bread which my Son is. He is Life in fiery Love. He rouses from sleep all who are dead in body or spirit. He dissolves sins into bright splendor, He, Who is Himself the rising life of holiness in us" (SC III, 1).

Chapter 4

The Human Being in the Cosmos

God composed the world from all its elements for the glory of his name. He strengthened the earth with winds, illumined her with stars and filled her with creatures of every kind. He thus surrounded and strengthened human beings with all there is in the world, giving them great power. All of creation was destined to be a helpmate for them, for human beings can neither live nor survive without the elements. (WM II, 2)

"Everything That Exists in the Order of God Responds to the Other"

The entire cosmos is meant to be God's dwelling place and our home, Hildegard tells us. The harmonious motions of its seasons, its winds, the sea, and the fertile earth are the music by which creation praises God, for "everything that exists in the order of God responds to the other" ("Omnia enim quae in institutione Dei sunt, sibi invicem responsum dant") (*Liber vitae meritorum*, in PI I, 14, n. 22, p. 68). We, human beings, create a dissonance in the sound of praise and response. We are not in touch with our true nature and live in the exile of unrelatedness.

The visions in Hildegard's *Liber vitae meritorum* (The Book of Life's Merits) speak about ethical decision human beings need to make for responsible involvements with the cosmos and history. According to Hildegard, we are responsible for much more than just our private life or the life of our soul. Human beings are responsible for one another, for their social and communal life, and for the well-being of the entire cosmos. Unfortunately, we have only the written word, no illuminations, for these visions.

In *Liber vitae meritorum* Hildegard reports that she "saw" and "heard" a conversation between the grieving elements and the figure of a man who filled the cosmos from the heights to the depths, a man whose attention gradually turned toward every direction. A kind of trumpet formed from a fiery cloud in front of his mouth. Every time he blew into it, three winds emerged. Each wind was overshadowed by a cloud. Sun and moon were in a cloud of light; the faithfully departed waited for their eternal home in a storm cloud; and a choir of fiery beings confronted the corrupt confusion of the world with the powers of God from a fiery cloud. This "Cosmic Man" is a personification of the triune God.

It is best to listen to this conversation between the grieving elements and the Cosmic Man not as an extraordinary visionary experience but as a deep truth that demands decisive choices even today:

> And I heard how the elements of the world turned to that man with a wild cry. And they shouted: "We cannot run any more to finish our course as our master willed it. For people with their evil deeds reverse our course, like a mill that turns everything upside down. We already reek like the pest and hunger for the fullness of justice."
>
> The Cosmic Man answered: "I will sweep you clean with my broom, and I will afflict the people until they turn back to me. In the meantime I will prepare many hearts and draw them to my heart.... Now all the winds are filled with the decay of leaves, and the air spits out pollution so that people can hardly open their mouths anymore. The greening life force [*viriditas*] has weakened because of the ungodly erring of deluded human souls. They follow only their own desires and shout: "Where is this God, whom we never get a chance to see?" (MV III, 2–3)

What deep insight into human nature Hildegard had! Hearing these words in a twentieth-century context, we immediately focus on her profound insight into "ecological" sin. We realize that she points to something that we now experience full-blown in the reality of acid rain, toxic wastes, dying forests, pollution, a damaged ozone layer, and the very real possibility of the end of life as we know it. Hildegard focused primarily on something else: on the fullness of justice for which the elements of the earth hunger and on the weakening of the greening life force, the *viriditas* of cosmic interrelatedness. This weakening is caused by human failure to know our place within an organic, interrelated universe, by our failure to know God and to know ourselves. But it can also be reversed by repentance, conversion, and the resulting social involvement.

The "hunger" Hildegard refers to is deeply related to St. Paul's statement that "all of creation groans as in childbirth waiting for the sons and daughters of God to be revealed" (Rom. 8:19). Our rationalistic, Enlightenment-conditioned approach to ecological problems fails to arouse the deep contemplative consciousness that knows this kind of "hunger" and groaning from experience. Hildegard would probably reprimand us for focusing *only* on observable facts in our efforts to save the environment, for grounding our interpretations of ourselves and of our universe in the bleak model of Newtonian physics. Like St. Benedict, she might urge us to "listen with the ears of the heart"; to look for the intricate beauty of the whole, where all is meant to be in relationship as a loving God ordained it; and to open the ears of our hearts to the reality of life on earth and to the Gospel. The enemies to unity and relatedness reside in human hearts and get solidified in structures.

Hildegard poses a challenge for each and every one of us today. Having lost the sense that the earth is part of an organically ordered cosmos, we have much to learn from the wisdom expressed in her visionary theology, which makes ecology a spiritual task and spirituality a powerful agent of social reform.

She would be a beacon for discoveries that are only now emerging in science, theology, and psychology, her remarkable insights into these sophisticated fields of knowledge always being bound to basic attitudes of seeking God: awe, reverence, humility, repentance, and prayer.

Were Hildegard alive in our age, she would have been at ease in conversations with Pierre Teilhard de Chardin, the French theologian and paleontologist who, like Hildegard, situates the individual human journey in a global and cosmic setting he calls the "divine milieu." Like Hildegard, he identifies Love as the driving energy that unites everything that is fragmented. New perspectives about our relationship to all of creation not only emerge from the contemplative consciousness of a twelfth-century woman but flow like a river throughout the centuries as Wisdom becomes ever more incarnate.

In our century, not only theologians like Teilhard de Chardin but also scientists see the world as a vast, living organism of which human beings are an integral part. Hildegard might have dialogued with Rupert Sheldrake about Love as the organizing principle of morphogenetic fields, organizational patterns that become concrete whenever the right conditions prevail. She might have written Fritjof Capra, who feels that the same fundamental unity and dynamic interrelatedness of the universe that science investigates is spoken of in different analogies by the mystics. She might have spoken with Carl Jung about the power of symbols and the reality of the archetypal realm, although Jung's wrestling with God led him to wrong conclusions when he speaks about a "dark side of God." She might have been very interested in David Bohm's cosmology, which posits an "implicate order" as the order that enfolds and unfolds all there is in the "explicate order." The living life force Hildegard calls *viriditas* would have been a point of connection in their conversations. Modern scientists might understand what Hildegard expressed in her antiphon to the Holy Spirit, although their terminology would differ (see illumination 3, "The Wheel of Life").

> The Spirit of God
> is a life that bestows life,
> root of the world tree
> and wind in its boughs.
>
> Scrubbing out sins,
> she rubs oil into wounds.
>
> She is glistening life
> alluring all praise,
> all-awakening,
> all resurrecting. (SY 141)

Illumination 3
The Wheel of Life

I can picture Hildegard actively involving herself in the Monastic Interreligious Dialogue, in the interaction between Christian contemplatives and contemplatives of other traditions who dialogue on the level of spiritual experience that unites them, even if their questions and insights into the Mystery of God differ. Hildegard fully realized that one's Christian identity is always in the process of being born. She would have known that the horizon of modern times makes it necessary to take the wisdom of the Rule of St. Benedict beyond the well-worn paths of the monastic community. As we approach the twenty-first century, global interdependence demands the pursuit of a common purpose and the rethinking of structures to meet new challenges. The United Nations could probably benefit from Hildegard's Benedictine focus on community in the widest sense as it struggles to meet challenges for peace and justice in an emerging global community. The political, economic, social, and environmental security of the human community is a challenge for rich and poor countries alike. It mandates sovereign states to recognize their interdependence and to become creative for the common good. *Viriditas* has a social component.

While emphasizing that creation was created as our helpmate, "for human beings can neither live nor survive without the elements," Hildegard calls us back to the biblical perspective that Scripture is the mirror of our identity. While God is the author of the fullness of justice for which the elements cry, this justice is forged in and through the earthen vessels of our humanity. Received as gift, it must be refined in human decisions and actions to mend a broken world. We have to face each particular situation and decide for or against relatedness. Gifted with consciousness, and also with discernment if the flame of God's Love burns brightly in our hearts, we need to stand at the crossroads of decision, as Hildegard calls it. In contemporary language we might say that we must be willing to live in the field of tension between two polarities. To freely choose the way of God — the tension-filled way of our true humanity — over conformity with the powers of sin and death will inevitably entail a kind of crucifixion. But the pains of confronting the lie, of facing self-deceptive systems of unrelatedness — both personal and social — are the birth pangs of the "new creation" if this earth is to become a true homeland for all:

> The earth grants sprouting fecundity according to the nature of human beings, depending on the quality and direction of their lives and actions. Men and women are the light-green heart of the living fullness of nature. A direct connection exists between the heart of a person and all the elements of the cosmos. They effect together that which has been decided in human hearts. (CB/LS 22)

Hildegard encourages us to see our responsibility for the cosmos and history in a larger framework. Heinrich Schipperges, a German Hildegard scholar, puts this framework into a very precise form: human beings are first of all the creation of God (*opus Dei*); they realize themselves in relationship (*opus alterum per alterum*); and they have an ecological and therapeutic task (*opus cum creatura*). Realizing ourselves in relationship does not only refer to relationships with another person or the larger human community in all its forms. Nature, according to Hildegard, is willing to cooperate with us, to give freely of its fecundity, of its life force. Hildegard's challenge to us is a call to become humble enough to understand our place in the universe and then to realize it in relationship. Embracing the ecological and therapeutic task of coming back into relationship with all there is will make us aware of both the dignity and the poverty of our being, as individuals and as communities: the dignity and glory of being human and the poverty of our failures. We have to start the healing process in the very place of alienation: "All creatures desire their creator;... only human beings are rebels, they alone tear the one creation apart into chaos."

Hildegard's challenge holds as true in the twentieth century as it did in the twelfth century. She invites us into an interior dialogue between the hard facts of reality and the perception of the transcendent mystery we call God. As a Benedictine, Hildegard tells us to "listen with the ears of the heart," to go beyond the gathering of facts, information, programs, and the resulting activities. She tells us that we are split at the core of our humanity. Factual information and intellectual understanding are no longer connected to the filter of emotional response for most of us. Likewise, emotional response to circumstances often lacks a framework of meaning and its articulation. A hectic activism that has nothing to do with truly creative work in and for this world results from this split.

As accurately as she diagnoses our alienated stance in this intended symphony of praise and response, Hildegard also reveals the therapy for its cure. She tells us that our true root and home are in the heart of God. In a vision (SC III, 1), she "sees" the human being as a much-loved lump of clay in the heart of the Creator:

> And I saw an immeasurably broad and high rock, the color of iron, with a white cloud above it. On it stood a round royal throne on which sat the Living One, shining in marvelous glory so brightly that I could not behold him clearly. In his breast he held something like a black, dirty clump of clay, the size of a heart of a grown-up person. It was surrounded by precious stones and pearls....(SC III, 1)

> In his breast, that is in the Wisdom of his Mystery, he carries a poor, weak, infirm lump of clay for love of his Son....This points to the unfolding of the deep and great wisdom in which God created the human. God looks out for all who are destined for liberation through the contrition of their soul, no matter what they may commit in their weakness while resisting God. They will come to God all the same. They are surrounded by jewels — those who rise among them like precious stones: martyrs and holy virgins — and pearls — the innocent and repentant children of salvation — with which the lump of clay is richly adorned. Great powers blaze up in the human body, powers which shine in God in brilliant glory. For he, who created the breath and life of human beings, looked at himself....(SC III, 1, 4)

> The Son of God, who went forth from the heart of the Father when he came into the world, is present to believers. They hold on to him with devoted fidelity. Therefore they appear in the breast of the gentle Father, so that no angel or other creature may spurn human beings, for the incarnate Son of the Most High took human nature into himself. (SC III, 1, 6)

With an embrace and a kiss the human being is released from the depth of God's heart and sent into the womb of this world. Made in the image of God, we are made out of the created elements of this world that God chose for his Incarnation. We are totally dependent on all species, but we are even more dependent on the deep desire for God, our mother. Our true home is the heart of God, which scintillates with life and motherly care. Hildegard tells us that we should neither look down on creation nor abandon it, for this would mean abandoning our Creator:

> Who thus trusts God will also honor the existing world, the course of sun and moon, the winds and air, the earth and water, everything that God created for the glory of human beings and for their protection. Human beings have no other ground to stand on. If they abandon this world, it will result in destruction by demons and dismissal from the protection of the angels. (WM II, 22)

But neither can we abandon our desire for God because that would mean abandoning our own deepest nature and potential. In a prayer to Jesus Christ, Hildegard expresses this boldly: "You, who suck on the breast of mercy and truth, I name my brother because of your Incarnation. God, who became my mother in my creation, nourishes humanity with this food, giving me life and growth" (SC II, 6, 35).

Our deep desire has gone astray. We, who are the greatest and most beloved work of God, and for whom he created the entire world, have a faltering, wavering, unsettled nature, Hildegard tells us. Our inclination is to say: "I know that I myself can do anything!" (SC I, 4) and forget that we need God's help to become genuinely creative. We are not in touch with our deep desire for God, with our true dignity, or with our true poverty. Only with inner eyes of faith can we see that the body, the soul, and the cosmos should be a dynamic, interdependent harmony that mirrors God and act out of that awareness. Our relationship to body, to nature, and to spirit or soul is distorted. Avoiding a real facing of our failures, we escape into projections or into autonomous action. Avoiding the taste of our deepest desire, we likewise escape into a desert of separated existence.

Fecundity (*Viriditas*)

Hildegard calls us back to a whole and integrated relatedness that has its root in the deep desire for God and in the human capacity to stand at the crossroads of decision and make a free and conscious choice for and in this world: a choice for the way of God and solidarity rather than for the powers of sin and death, a choice for the way that leads to fecundity (*viriditas*) of cosmos and history rather than for a way that leads to aridity and a shriveling into barrenness. We do not have to despair over the overwhelming problems that confront the human community at the end of the twentieth century. Hildegard never ceases to remind us that we have tremendous power. Although each human being is seemingly small and insignificant within the structure of our historical reality, each one can become very capable. If each of us opens the depth of our heart to the Mystery of God in the concrete events of life, and then — in freedom — decides for the good, then fecundity of cosmos and nature will proceed from this very personal act. Hildegard is very specific about the functioning, activity, and effects of the power of fecundity, the living life force of *viriditas*. In an analogical way she describes how it is inherent and operating in all of creation, and specifically in the vitality of the human heart, intellect, and conscience. *Viriditas* operates in the structure of the human body, in its metabolism and its states of illness and health, which are all influenced by the constellation of specific months in the course of the year (WM IV). For Hildegard the human being — body and soul — is a microcosm of the great cosmos and is meant to be a creative member of the circle of life on this precious earth. Each personal decision affects all of us. It can contribute either to the healing of the planet or to a further shriveling up in separation, hopelessness, fear, and pollution. We are responsible not only to God and to each other but also to the elements.

Hildegard's theological paradigm for our task is the mystery of the dying and rising Christ, the Wisdom of God. This Christic dynamic of dying and rising in everyday life, which is forged through grace by individuals in community, on this earth, is what is meant by *viriditas*, fecundity. In it we experience the embrace of "God's maternal love which nourishes us into life" (SC II, 2, 4). *Viriditas* expresses growth in fertility in all its forms, which is always experienced as opposed by or in tension with *ariditas,* a shriveling into barrenness.

Viriditas and related terms form a whole spectrum of meanings in Hildegard's work. Contrary to other Hildegardian symbols, it is a nonbiblical term that arose from the depth of her feminine psyche, through which the experience of the mystery of Christ was filtered. On a deep spiritual level she experienced the revelation that in the fire of God's love Christ permeates all levels of reality: the cosmos, the human community, the divinity, all of eternity, and also all of time and history. The term *viriditas* arose from the very depth of this woman before God who was called to make all levels of Christ's presence explicit. She experienced grace like a mother experiences the movement of her yet-unborn child in the womb. Forging the term *viriditas,* Hildegard connected her female experience of awakening, call, and growth in fecundity as a prophetic woman with the work of the Cosmic Christ as the source and direction of history. The term differs from the abstract theological terms we are used to. It functions as a symbol that informs and organizes Hildegard's theology and spirituality. True symbols always give rise to thought. The term *viriditas,* fecundity in all its forms, can ground the faith and hope of fellow God-seekers in a common cosmos of meaning and the lived experience of Christic *viriditas.*

Viriditas, fecundity as the work of Christ, points not only to the greening power of creation and the potential of true human fecundity in cosmos and history. It also points to the inner life of God, the endless circling of love and total response described as the Trinity. For Hildegard this was the most important reality, preceding and continually supporting all other forms of fecundity. Hildegard's unusual Trinitarian images are a flaming eye of Love, whose pupil is a blessing Christ figure (SC II, 2), and a three-edged purplish-black column, which represents the unity of the Father with his fruitful Word who redeemed us and with the Holy Spirit who helps us to give witness (SC II, 7). This reality is the column of all good, which pervades creation and history, and its three edges function like blades that cut through all lack of faith, self-sufficiency, and separation.

The inner life of God, an ever-circling Love and interdependent response, entered this world not through humanity in general but through one specific woman, Mary. Through her consent it took up residence in her womb. Mary heard with the "ears of her heart" — she saw, she felt, she nurtured, she stood by, she suffered. Hildegard calls Mary the *virdisssima virga*, the most fruitful branch:

> Alleluia! light
> burst from your untouched
> womb like a flower
> on the farther side
> of death. The world-tree
> is blossoming. Two
> realms become one. (SY 125)

Two realms have become one, through Mary. Now all of us, men and women, are called to listen with the "ears of the heart." Are we willing to be penetrated and transformed by the fiery Love of God? Are we willing to bear the interdependence and responsiveness of the God-reality in the wombs of our being for the good of this world? Religious experience comes through the feminine mode of being, as Ann Ulanov points out:

> It comes through the matrix of the unconscious, unfathered by any conscious skill, neither created nor authorized by any cultural intent of anything else that we could claim as our doing. It comes through the dark mothering unconscious of our being. It comes through the feminine as one-in-herself, as virgin, that capacity in us to receive the transcendent each time as for the first time. (*The Wisdom of the Psyche*, 99)

Hildegard was very aware that we, like Mary, need to become God-bearers.

It is not easy for modern people to enter into the rich realm of symbolic thinking that permeates Hildegard's writings, but Hildegard herself tells us that she found "biblical symbols and images more suitable to teach divine things than the naked word." In *Scivias*, Hildegard reports hearing the voice from heaven: "All these things are so hidden in my Mystery that human senses and understanding cannot plumb the breadth and the depth of it unless I grant that understanding" (SC III, 2, 28). This is not an anti-intellectual statement but merely a recognition of the limits of human knowledge in the face of mystery. Theology, speaking about God, cannot be divorced from an experiential knowledge of God, and this experience is most often spoken of in symbolic language. Experiential knowledge of God, rooted in Scripture and tradition, was the entryway to theology for Hildegard. In her age, symbolic interpretation was also the dominant approach to the reading of Scripture. Many central scriptural symbols like the Exodus, Jerusalem, and the Genesis text "Let there be light" were interpreted on four levels.

Assuming that for Hildegard the term *viriditas* had become a profound theological symbol that arose from the depth of her experience and points to God's relatedness to creation and history, let me indicate briefly how Hildegard used the medieval exegetical model. She leads her readers to four levels of insight that illuminate the finite in all its possibilities. On the literal level, the multivalent symbol *viriditas* points to the fecundity of all creation. On the allegorical level, *viriditas* points to the human body as the microcosm of the macrocosm. Tropologically, *viriditas* has to do with the form of the risen Christ — reverberating in the very marrow of body and soul — in history and creation. On the anagogical or mystical level, *viriditas* points to the world of complete insight, the world of eternity and peace, of Christ in glory.

Does Hildegard's symbolic term *viriditas* bring our own religious experience of God to expression? Does it somehow reveal, clarify, and disclose who we are in relation to our God, in relation to life on this earth? Like her spiritual father St. Benedict, Hildegard calls us to listen with the "ears of the heart" to the hidden light and sound of God's presence among us. We do not have to be Benedictines to do this.

Embraced by the Maternal Love of God

To put flesh on our little discourse on symbolic thinking, let us go back to Hildegard's texts. For Hildegard, a powerful, overwhelming vision revealed the intended cosmic interrelatedness and responsibility to which the symbol *viriditas* points. In the second vision of her cosmology, *De operatione Dei*, Hildegard "sees" the entire cosmos with all its elements and the human being in its center as embraced by the blood-red, fiery circle of the Cosmic Christ, as a living organ in the body of God (see illumination 4). There are images of polarities in tension: the cosmos as the giant moving wheel of history, embraced by God's glowing love, wondrously ordered with the elements, the stars and the earth as its axis. A towering human being stands cruciform in the center of tension and within an intricate web of rays that are connected to the elements and the stars, the human being moving the web like a net with his hands:

> And finally you see that a light that is brighter than the clearest day emerges like a gossamer net from the mouth of the described figure [the Cosmic Christ] in whose breast the cosmic wheel appears. From the primordial source of real Love, in whom the cosmic order rests, shines her exceedingly precise ordering of all things. It comes to light in ever new ways, holding and tending everything there is. (WM II, 46)

In this visionary image the figure of a human being fills the entire cosmic wheel, surrounded by the cosmic circles of the elements and winds, which penetrate and enliven the entire body. The human being towers over the dark globe of the earth, indicating the cosmic stature and responsibility of each and every human being. Hildegard explains how she experienced the God-intended collaboration of human beings with the cosmos:

> The human stands in the center of the cosmos as more important than the other creatures, who remain dependent on the cosmic structure. The human is small in stature yet great in the power of soul. With raised head and feet firmly planted on the ground, the human can affect things above and below. Whatever the right or left hand produces penetrates the universe because — in the power of their inmost humanity — human beings have the ability to achieve this. For just as the human body surpasses the heart in size, so are the powers of the soul greater than those of the body. Just as the heart is hidden in the human body, so is the body surrounded by the powers of the soul because these reach to the ends of the earth. Thus faith-filled people have their being in knowing God and seek God in worldly and spiritual needs.... For

Illumination 4
The Cosmos in the Womb of God

just as the eyes of the body see creation on all sides, so do the eyes of faith see the Lord everywhere. It is God whom the human recognizes in every creature, knowing He created all there is. (DW II, 15)

Are we easily in touch with this deep truth? No, Hildegard reminds us in the "Son of Man Speech" in *Scivias:*

O you foolish people, lukewarm and shameless you shrink into yourselves, and do not want to open even one eye to see what you really are in the integrity of your spirit. On the contrary, you intend to do the evil your flesh desires and you refuse to have a good conscience and the right spiritual view. You act as if you had no understanding of good and evil, nor the honor to know how to avoid evil and to do good. Listen to me, the Son of Man, who speaks to you: O human being, reflect on what you were when you were just coagulating in your mother's womb. You were without knowledge and power when you were called to life. But then spirit, and motion, and sense perception were given to you so that you would move lively and in moving would recognize the fruit of usefulness. (SC III, 10, 1)

This speech takes as its first topic the human being, reminding us that human beings are the key to the structure of nature, history, and even the economy of salvation. The structure and intent of our hearts influence the structure of this world. The discernment of what is good or evil is constitutive of our true nature. It is hidden by our fragility, which we encounter on our search for God, on the journey into our true self. Hildegard shows us many facets of this fragility, which she describes as a shriveling up of our true potential into uselessness for God, the world, and all intended relatedness. Yet she also reminds us of the constant admonishment of the Holy Spirit, who permeates even our alienation with a recollection of true discernment. But we need to ask, to pray for this freedom of the children of God. Hildegard "heard" the following words in the "Son of Man Speech," which asks us to retrieve the treasure that is hidden in the field of our hearts:

This is how your creator builds. He gave you a most precious treasure, namely a vibrant understanding, for he greatly delights in you because you are his creation. He instructed you through the words of the law, which he instituted, to use this very understanding to bring profit in good works and to be rich in virtues, so that through this the good giver of gifts would be more accurately known. You must therefore contemplate always in which way the great gift you received — to be used for others as well as for yourself — brings forth the brilliance of holiness, so that people, called forth by your example, give honor and praise to God because of it. If you multiply it profitably in all justice, the praise and thanksgiving will stretch toward a knowledge of God who has inflamed these virtues in you through the power of the Holy Spirit. He will turn to you in the compassion of his grace, and through the sweetness of his delight he will set you aflame in a firestorm of love for him. Filled with the consolation of the Holy Spirit you will wisely discern all that is good, and you will do even greater works. Burning with love, you will glorify your Father who has kindly granted this to you.

May my sheep hear these, my very words, and may whoever has the ears of the interior spirit heed them! For it pleases me that people who know and love me should be busy in such a way that — affected by the gifts of the Holy Spirit — they interiorly understand how to act. (SC III, 10, 9)

How do we learn to listen with "ears of the interior spirit"? How do we become all eyes for the God-reality that is unseen yet pervades all there is? How do we learn to become "the light-green heart of the fullness of nature"? That will be the focus of another chapter.

Chapter 5

The Union of
Body and Soul

The soul is like a wind that waves over herbs,
Is like the dew that moistens the grass
Is like the rain-soaked air that lets things grow.

In the same way you should radiate kindness
To all who are filled with longing.

Be a wind, helping those in need.
Be a dew, consoling the abandoned.
Be the rain-soaked air, giving heart to the weary,
Filling their hunger with instruction
By giving them your soul. (HK 306)

Nowadays there is much interest in the soul. We talk about
"loss of the soul," "care of the soul," about soul friends, soul
food, and music that has soul. Many of us are aware that we inherited a spirituality that separates body and soul, that sees the
body as something to be tamed and controlled by the soul. In
Hildegard's writings we do not find such dualism. Correspond-
ing to her view of the cosmos, Hildegard describes body and
soul as partners, both dependent on and supportive of the other.
"Wherever body and soul live in genuine harmony, there the
highest reward is gained in unanimous joy" (WM IV 2). During life on earth, body and soul are meant to be inseparably
united. How did Hildegard overcome the inherited dualism?
Through her own experience of the mystery — and by daring
to name the new sense of herself, of God, of the cosmos, and of
the unity of body and soul. She mirrors for us a deep truth in
which we can see more clearly the truth of our own lives. We

have become blind to the profound interrelatedness that should be the pattern of all there is. We have become blind to the true potential of our humanity:

> And God created the human being according to God's image and likeness with the intent to clothe the holy divinity with this very form. For this reason God inscribed all of creation in the human form, just as likewise the entire world emerged from God's Word. (WM IV, 14)

> In the fullness of grace the Word created the universe in his divinity and redeemed it in his humanity. (WM IV, 105)

As exemplary beings who can mirror this deep truth, we should be "all eyes" for the God-reality that resides in the depth of our being. But we have forgotten our true origin and have to painfully walk the "way of the heart" into our fragility, brokenness, and unrelatedness before we can return home: home into our body, home into this world, home into all of creation, home into the human community, home to God.

The soul has a bridging function in the "re-membering," in this "re-creation" of connectedness, according to Hildegard. It is the soul's task to be the body's beloved partner, to help it express its true task on earth:

> The soul has two capacities which overcome both strains and the repose of her passionate labors with the very same power. With one capacity she rises to the heights where she feels God, with the other she takes possession of the entire body in which she lives in order to accomplish her work together with the body. For it is the soul's joy to become effective in the body. She strives forever to perfect the work of the body that was created by God. (WM IV, 19)

> The soul is the greening life-force [*viriditas*] of the flesh, for the body grows and prospers through her, just as the earth becomes fruitful when it is moistened. The soul humidifies the body so it does not dry out, just like the rain which soaks into the earth. (WM IV, 21)

Hildegard gives us a rich bouquet of metaphors for the work of the soul with and in the body: not only moisture but also breath and even bright-burning understanding, *rationalitas*. This is another one of Hildegard's key terms. It does not refer to the rational intellect as we generally understand it but rather points to an ever-deeper and ever-deepening process of understanding what the transformation in Love entails. It speaks to the human capacity to be open to God and to the painful/joyous work of reuniting what has been separated:

> When the Word of God sounded, it appeared in every crea-ture, and this sound was the life in every creature. The same Word is the source for works of the human spirit. The same sound is the source of bright-burning understanding [*ratio-nalitas*], which brings forth her works, in sounds of song or calling. Likewise, in the clarity of her artistic ability, she calls forth the sounds of musical instruments in every creature. Made in the image and likeness of God, the human being is gifted with bright-burning understanding through the liv-ing soul, and the soul attracts the flesh with its glowing fire. (WM IV, 105)

> The soul is rational spirit. She lives in the house of the heart with her wisdom, which ponders and orders everything like the father of a family who wisely orders the affairs of his house.... The soul is of fiery nature. She warms all the life events she brings to her heart and cooks them to unity. (WM IV, 25)

> Just as the wind ignites a firebrand, so does bright-burning understanding move and illuminate the human soul. The power of understanding moves in the soul like the wind, is like the light of the fire. And the soul is a breath, sent by God into the human, a breath which never wanes and which is rational. And just as the fire would not be a fire without the glow, so the soul would have no insight without bright-burning understanding. (WM IV, 27)

The fiery, vivifying, bright-burning kind of understanding that Hildegard describes as the soul's nature needs the body just as much as the body needs the soul:

> The soul assists the flesh and the flesh, the soul. For every single work is perfected through soul as well as flesh, so that the soul is revived by doing good and holy works with the

flesh. But the flesh is often irked when co-operating with the soul, and so the soul stoops to the level of the flesh and allows it to take delight in some deed, just as a mother causes her weeping child to laugh. And in this way, the flesh performs some good works with the soul, but mixed together with certain sins which the soul tolerates so that the flesh is not oppressed. For just as the flesh lives through the soul, so too, the soul is revived by doing good works with the flesh, because the soul has been stationed inside the works of the Lord's hands. In the same way that the sun, overcoming night, climbs until the middle of the day, so a human being, too, rises up, by avoiding corrupt deeds. And just as the sun declines in the afternoon, so too, the soul makes accord with the flesh. And as the moon is rekindled by the sun so that it does not disappear, so the flesh of a person is sustained by the powers of the soul, so that it does not go to ruin. (WM IV, 24)

Union of body and soul — a true partnership of the two is needed to work with and in God for the good of this world:

The soul is in the body as the sap is in the tree; and the powers of the soul are like the figure of the tree. How is this so? Understanding in the soul is like the green vigour of the branches and leaves of the tree. Will is like the flowers on the tree; mind like the first fruit bursting forth. But reason is like the fruit in the fullness of maturity; while sense is like the height and spread of the tree. And in the same way, the human body is strengthened and supported by the soul. (SC I, 4, 26)

The soul inhabits her body with great care, like the father of a family in his house. She is always concerned that nothing good be lacking. (WM IV, 71)

In the partnership of body and soul the soul will vivify, warm, water, enflame, and cook the body in the fire of Love to prepare the human being to stand — with others — on the crossroads of decision for and in this world. We are capable of perceiving with the bright-burning understanding, with the will, and with all the senses of our body that we are meant to cooperate with God for the good of this world. For this task, discernment (*discretio*), a right balance, is needed, and that is hard to achieve. Hildegard invites her readers to enter into this lifelong process:

> Human beings reach perfection in the flowering of childhood and early adulthood. Then in old age they go into withered decline, just as in summer the earth is adorned as it blossoms in greenness, and then in winter turns pale with the cold. For when the soul has so overcome the body that it accords with it in simple heart and good will, and is delighted with good works as though with some delicious food, that person says in heavenly desire, "How sweet are the declarations of your justice in my throat. To my mouth too they are far sweeter than honey." And so with a child's simplicity, that person lives in innocence, without fleshly desire. But the soul so steeps that one in these desires that the person grows green in the ascent from virtue to virtue, and blossoms in the good works and example that the Son of God has left us. For being untainted by the malice of sins, that person rejoices within and is adorned. And just as in the cold of winter, the blossoming and maturing of all fruits fail, so in death human beings fail in all their works, both good and bad. But the person who, in infancy, childhood, and old age has completed good works happily — his soul, shining with these same works and, as it were, adorned with precious stones, climbs into the presence of God; and the body, which performed these works through the soul, can scarcely wait until they abide together in the mansion of joy. (WM IV, 78)

> The soul suffuses the entire body just like the power of the winds storm through the entire universe. For the soul, which was sent into the body by the Spirit of God, totally penetrates the entire organism with her powers. Just as the blowing winds roar through the firmament, so does the soul entice the human being to love God in the most ardent way and to do those works which conform to holiness. These works have the taste of dripping honey, for the words of the Lord drip from his mouth sweeter than honey and honeycomb. (WM IV, 50)

Sent by the Spirit of God into the body, the soul thus vivifies and aids the body, leading it to come to know God in faith and good works. Body and soul are meant to be true partners who have different tasks but depend on each other to bring each other to a fullness of mutuality and joy.

The Journey of the Soul

A vision in *Scivias* (SC I, 4) depicts the journey of the soul in and with the body (see illumination 5). Coming from the heart of the mystery into the body, the soul finds itself in the exile of alienation and strives to return from the way of error to her true homeland. Hildegard "sees" a golden kite-shaped figure, flaming, with many open eyes illuminating the star-filled sky. Its flaming brilliance signifies the Mystery of God's eternal counsel, which extends its gaze to the four corners of the earth and clearly sees all good and evil. Within its brilliance a center panel shines like the dawn with the brightness of blood-red fireballs and a skull. From this very center of God's eternal counsel, redemption in Christ, a golden stream flows into an egg-shaped image below it. Like an umbilical cord, it connects the Mystery of God's eternal counsel and a human fetus in the womb of a woman who is surrounded by a variety of figures. When the baby moves actively, according to divine design, a fireball seems to possess its heart, mind, and members, empowering the soul to act in and with the body like the sap in a tree. This fireball, the soul, does not have an easy journey in and with the body:

> When this human form, which had been thus empowered, emerged from the woman's womb, it changed color depending on the movement the fireball made within it. And I saw how many storms assailed such a fireball in the human body and weighed it down to the ground. But, gaining strength and raising itself up, it bravely resisted the storms and said with a groan:
> "A stranger, where am I? In the shadow of death. Which path am I traveling? The path of error. What consolations do I have? The consolation of the pilgrim in exile. I am meant to have a tent adorned with five stars more brilliant than the

xxx ʮ erba di ad hommes.ꝙ diuinuʃ p̄ceptuʃ obediaſ ꞇ malũ abicientes. bonũ ꝺ amore
dei fideliter perficiant. xxxvi. Ɗe fide catholica. xxxvii ʮ erba ysaiɤ ·

Illumination 5
The Journey of the Soul

sun and the stars.... I should have been a companion of the angels, for I am the living breath, which God sent into the dry loam. An thus I should know and sense God." (SC I, 4, 1)

The strip on the right side of illumination 5 has to be read from bottom to top as the soul's journey on earth. Created in God's image we are born into the land of alienation from relatedness and finitude. Slaves to the human drive for autonomy, or to reluctance to becoming who we can be, we experience this world like a winepress or an attack by wild beasts... until the soul awakens to God's grace, cries out to "Mother Zion" for help, and is given power to return home, to the body, to this world, to God. Hildegard's terms are more poetic and biblical than the modern language I just used: "We live like strangers in exile," " in the shadow of death," "at the crossroads of sorrow," and long for "our true homeland," which we see only in the "mirror of faith" and gain through remorse and good works. Hildegard often used the parable of the Prodigal Son to point to the way home, the way out of the land of forgetfulness and alienation, out of separation from God, from each other, from our own humanity. But she tells also us that the first desire of the soul is to return to "Mother Zion," a feminine side of the Divine Mystery.

"Woman Is Created for Man and Man Is Made for Woman"

Not only body and soul but also man and woman are meant to be true partners — not in the abstract but as concrete human beings who live — as man or as woman — in a specific historical context, relationship, and body. "Male and female he created them," the Genesis account tells us. Man and woman were not created as solitary beings but as the ones who would recognize each other as flesh of their flesh and bone of their bone, as the ones who are capable of friendship and total surrender to each other, as the ones who are capable of life-giving acts in its many forms.

Although Hildegard lived a celibate lifestyle, her visionary experiences taught her much about the God-intended complementary and interdependent relatedness of men and women.

Modifying 1 Cor. 11:9 ("For the man was not created for the woman but the woman for the man"), Hildegard interprets St. Paul through her own lens of interdependent fecundity:

> Thus it is written: Woman is created for man and man is made for woman, since as she is made from man and man from her, neither is separated from the other in the unity of producing offspring, because they produce one thing in a single work just as air and wind are all involved in the work of the other. (SC I, 2, 12)

Hildegard even argues that the interdependence of men and women in complementary roles can mirror the incarnational/redemptive pattern, that it can reach what the mystics called the spiritual marriage. It can be expressed in the physical love of a man and a woman within the radical surrender and fidelity of marriage. Hildegard tells us.

> God gave the man a helpmate in the form of a woman, a mirror image so to speak, in whom the entire human race was already latently present.... Man and woman are co-mingled in such a way that each one is the work of the other (opus alterum per alterum). Without the woman the man could not be called "man," without the man the woman could not be called "woman." Woman takes her being from man and man is a source of consolation for woman, and neither of them can henceforth live without the other. Man signifies the divinity of the Son of God and woman his humanity. Thus human beings sit on the judgment seat of the world. Every creature is under their cultivation and stands in their service. The human being is more than all the other creatures. (WM IV, 100)

A daring theological passage! Man and woman, together, can signify the divinity and humanity that were united in the Son of God. Hildegard speaks of woman as symbol for the humanity of Christ as life-bearer in the deepest sense if — in a fundamental interdependence with man — she becomes who she can be while helping man to become who he can be.

This bold statement has to be seen against the background of Hildegard's time. Woman was generally portrayed as vulnerable to sin, as temptress, as less rational than man; or she was revered as the virgin. Hildegard was socialized by a culture and a church that associated women with the sinful body and thus depreciated her role in representing the glory of creation as well as the power of redemption. Hildegard stepped out of this pattern. We cannot read her insights into the role of women in true partnership with men from a contemporary feminist perspective that pinpoints misogynist attitudes and patterns and is committed to changing consciousness and structures that reinforce women's subordination. Hildegard's insights arose from the consciousness of a heart and mind transformed by the cleansing fire of the Eternal Light. An experience like that, by its nature, demands an often difficult but hope-filled involvement in history.

Speaking the truth about her life, the truth about what she experienced of the divine reality, was neither easy, instantaneous, nor without suffering and doubt for Hildegard. It happened slowly, over the span of many years, as she gradually accepted her God-given task. In *Scivias* she speaks about her interior battle to accept the visionary experiences of God, about her task to pronounce them not only as her own truth but as a truth for all the people of God, as theology:

> Even though I "heard" and "saw" all this, I refused to write, not out of obstinacy, but because of the suspicion, the prejudices, and the ambiguity of human words in the service of humility. (SC, prologue)

> And suddenly the One enthroned upon the mountain called out with a loud and penetrating voice: "O fragile human being, made out of clay of the earth, ashes, from ashes, proclaim the way to eternal redemption so that all those are taught who know the inner meaning of the Scriptures but do not dare to speak or proclaim it. For they are lukewarm and superficial in the observation of divine justice. Open up to them the sealed mysteries which they conceal fearfully in a hidden and barren field. Pour yourself out like an overflowing fountain, flow out in mysterious teaching, so that the torrent of your flood will startle those which would like to punish you (as a woman) with contempt because of the transgressions of Eve." (SC I, 1)

And I heard the One who sat on the throne saying to me, "Write what you see and hear!" From the inmost knowledge of that vision I replied, "I implore you, my Lord, grant me understanding so that I may be able to give expression to these mystical things. Forsake me not, but strengthen me in the dawn of your inbreaking justice in which your Son revealed himself. Grant me to know how I can and should proclaim the divine plan which was ordained in the eternal counsel: how your Son was meant to take on flesh and become a human being within time. Before all of creation you simply willed in the fire of the dove, the Holy Spirit, that your Son should rise like the brilliant sun in the dawn of virginity, and be clothed with true humanity for humankind's sake." . . .

And again I heard it spoken to me: "Speak as you have been taught. I want you to speak although you are ashes from ashes. Speak to reveal the bread which the Son of God is. He is life in fiery love. He rouses from sleep all who are dead in body or spirit. He dissolves sins into bright splendor, he who is himself the rising life of holiness in us." (SC III, 1)

In addition to her own reluctance and fears to proclaim the mysteries of God, Hildegard encountered exterior obstacles. The opposition of the Benedictine monks to the foundation of her own monastery, for instance, or the generally accepted idea that "learned" men were the only ones who should speak about God, who should do theology, are two examples. Every time Hildegard hesitated to speak about the mystery of God's presence among us, every time she refused to speak the truth she knew from the depth of her being, she fell ill. She must have been afraid: afraid to be different from everybody else, afraid of self-deception, afraid to surrender all — heart, mind, body, actions, and relationships — to the living God. How does one speak about visions in which the Mystery of God is revealed "as in a mirror darkly"? How does one speak about reality where things are seen — all of a sudden — from the perspective of God? Like many before her and like many today, Hildegard tried to escape from her call to speak. Finally she dared to live in the tension of having no human security, of becoming "a feather on the breath of God." She dared to live consciously as a weak and unlearned woman whose authority came from God alone. She now could hold open house for all who came seeking advice and counsel because Wisdom had set up her tent in the depth of her being.

Hildegard had become relational and interdependent. For her this did not happen with one man but with all, men and women, who came to her seeking counsel. An example will help explain this. Wibert of Gembloux, a learned monk, had heard about Hildegard's fame and wrote her asking to please describe her visionary experiences. Hildegard, who was seventy at that time, responded with the famous letter, quoted in earlier chapters, in which she describes the mode of her visionary experiences (BR 226–28). The fact that she opened the depth of her being to a total stranger is quite extraordinary. Did this openness result from her visionary ability to discern the pure heart of the writer, or was it an attitude that rested in consent to a God-intended relatedness? When Hildegard's response arrived, Wibert did not dare open the letter at once. He put it on the altar of a nearby church and prayed for a pure heart. When he finally read it, he became ecstatic with joy. The next day Wibert read the letter to an assembly of clergy and laity. The abbot, Rupert von Königsberg, exclaimed:

> These words must be inspired by the Holy Spirit. The sharp-witted French masters do not produce anything like this.... With dry hearts and blown-up cheeks they produce a great clamor, they lose themselves in analysis and controversy.... But this blessed woman...emphasizes the one necessary thing, namely the honor of the triune God. She draws from her inner fullness and pours it out to quench the thirst of all who are thirsty. (BR 226)

Hildegard's insights into the intended partnership of men and women has to be seen against the background that she herself, although not in relationship with one specific man, had become fully relational. Her insights into intended mutuality and complementarity differ from the cultural and theological assumptions of her time. They have their source in the relational life of God that Hildegard experienced — as in a mirror darkly — in her visions. Her symbolic theological articulation of the relational, outpouring nature of God stands in the Emanation tradition. Her task became to pour herself out in a pattern that mirrors the divine reality, so that men and women might find a fuller life, with each other, in God.

"So God created humankind in his image, in the image of God he created them; male and female he created them" (Gen. 1:27–28). Commenting on this passage, Hildegard writes about God's intent for male/female relatedness in the following way:

> God created the human, namely man, as a being of greater strength, woman, however, of softer strength. He ordered the forms of both of them in the right measure of length and breadth and depth in all their members, just as God has ordered the length and breadth and depth of the other creatures in the right proportion so that not one of them would infringe improperly on another. (WM V, 93)

Hildegard "saw" that woman was created from the side of man, not from his rib. In a vision about the fall (SC I, 2), the tempter is shown blowing poisonous, dense fumes at a shining wing filled with stars that protrudes from Adam's side. This wing symbolizes Eve, who carries all of potential humanity in her womb. Lucifer, the great deceiver, wanted the sin of deception and unrelatedness to become incarnate, Hildegard tells us. He therefore targeted Eve in her life-giving potential when Adam and Eve walked in the innocence of Paradise. Looking at this symbolic image one could say that Hildegard sees woman as "the other side" of man, as complementary rather than inferior, as life-giver together with Adam. Although human beings have lost their equilibrium after the fall (Adam is shown sideways in this vision), the disrupted relatedness to all there is can become restored through grace and human cooperation.

Hildegard tells us that the uniting, attracting, and life-giving force of love between man and woman is meant to become a mirror image of the endlessly circling Love and response in the inner life of God, which desires to become present in history as fecundity in its many forms. Historical fecundity, *viriditas*, is the work of Christ, which needs our response and cooperation. Hildegard speaks about Adam and Eve's creation and God-intended relatedness in the following words:

> When God created Adam and then let him fall asleep, Adam became aware of a strong feeling of love while he was sleeping. And God created a form for the love of the man, and

thus woman is the love of the man. As soon as the woman was formed, God gave the man procreative potency, so that through his love, namely the woman, he could beget sons. When Adam looked at Eve, Wisdom fully entered his being, for he saw Eve as the mother through whom he was meant to beget sons. But when Eve looked at Adam, she gazed at him in such as way as if she could perceive heaven. The soul, which desires heaven, strains toward the heights. For her hope was focused on the man. Thus only one love and not any other ought to grow between man and woman.

...The great love which was in Adam when Eve emerged from him, and the sweetness of sleep in which he had rested, changed after the fall into the opposite of that sweetness. But because the man still senses this great sweetness in himself, he runs swiftly like a deer to running waters to the woman and the woman to him. (HW 172)

The tension of opposites between man and woman that manifests in sexual desire and love is so highly appreciated by Hildegard that she puts it — contrary to tradition — on equal par with the monastic "desire for heaven" and a life of virginity. Man and woman in their sexual union and begetting of children can become co-creators with God. From their union arise future generations who — in faith and hope — might bring about that fecundity of history that reveals the Kingdom-reality. Man and woman together make visible who the human being is. Man and woman together, not separate, were created in the image and likeness of God. Their love and actions can mirror the Love of God: "God united the woman to the man with an oath of fidelity, in such a way that the fidelity between them should never be broken. They are rather to be partners like body and soul which God joined together as one" (WM I, 15).

Hildegard always shows us two sides of reality, the God-intended, hidden side of reality, and reality as it is experienced — by wounded, fear-filled psyches — in an imperfect world. Although man and woman do not live the perfection of complementarity and relatedness Hildegard describes as their God-given potential, the energies of God's grace (*virtutes*) continually surround and encourage them to reach for their graced potential. Hildegard knows, and in our age we are certainly aware of this fact, that sexuality is often encountered as lust or is desired for its own sake, that relationships are often needy, abusive, and not life-giving. Hildegard would nevertheless ask men and women to live in the constant tension between the many modes of fecundity and barrenness in their relationship; she would ask them to live in the constant tension between life-giving and life-denying modes of presence to each other. She would remind them that as true partners in body and soul they are meant to mirror the fecundity that gives life to this world. But this can only happen with the help of God.

In the sections of Hildegard's works devoted to explaining the man/woman relationship we again find her unusual term *rationalitas* as a key component. It points to the human capacity to be open to God and to one another in the task of reuniting what had been separated. Hildegard always refers to very concrete situations in which responsible action arises from this potential and the gift of rational, loving discernment. Talking about sexual arousal Hildegard says:

> In them [the sexual organs] the gift of bright-burning understanding (*rationalitas*) also flourishes, so that human beings know what to do or not to do. Therefore they find joy in the sexual act, which is warmed and strengthened on the body's right side through the human breath and by the liver. In this way the human becomes reverent and disciplined. (WM III, 1)

Hildegard never fails to remind us that our deep desire for God and for one another has gone astray, that the gift of bright-burning understanding is often hidden under the evasions, self-reliance, and distortions that are the mode in which our faltering, unsettled nature approaches reality. We forget that we need God's help; we forget that we are not really in touch with our deep desire for God, with our true dignity; we forget that we are not really in touch with our true poverty. In the concrete events of a man/woman relationship, healing and genuine relatedness become possible through the embrace and acknowledgment of personal woundedness, aridity, and estrangement from our true nature, from the source of life. Woundedness that is shown to God and to each other can take many shapes, each one revealing a desire to step out of the exile of God-forgetfulness. According to Hildegard, Christ is the great physician to whom we need to bring our wretchedness, wounds, and sins. In the "Exhortation to Married People" in the "Son of Man Speech" in *Scivias*, Hildegard refers to this ability to return from the exile of unrelatedness that is the exile of God-forgetfulness:

> You have been given great perception; great judgment is therefore demanded of you. You have received much, and much will be asked of you. But in all this I am your head and your helper. Whenever you call out to me — touched by the heavenly touch — you will hear an answer from me. If you knock on the door, it will be opened for you. In the spirit of the most pointed perception which is given to you, you have everything you need within yourself. Because you have this within you, my sharp and perceptive eyes will look at what they find within you.
>
> In your conscience I seek the wounds and pains of your heart; through them you should restrain yourself whenever you sense that your will pulls you toward sin and you are so enflamed by it that — totally liquefied — you hardly are able to breathe. Behold, I look at you; what will you do? When you call out to me in this labor with a wounded heart, eyes moistened by tears, and shaken by fear of my judgment, and when you persevere in calling out to me that I may hasten to help you, . . . then I will do all you desire and will make my dwelling place in you. (SC III, 10, 3)

Men and women become capable of friendship and total surrender in love — they become capable of being life-givers in the widest sense — whenever they travel the journey of acknowledging their alienation and of embracing their potential for true partnership. This is the healing journey home into God-intended complementarity.

Chapter 6

The Way of the Heart
(*Iter cordis*)

Only the way of the heart (*iter cordis*) leads us home to God, Hildegard tells us. But it must be traveled with others and with all of creation. Caecilia Bonn, OSB, a German Hildegard scholar at the Abbey St. Hildegard, has explored Hildegard's way of the heart. She has pointed out three steps on the journey home into God.

First Step: Remembering

The first step is a profound remembering of who we truly are. Hildegard calls this step *recordatio* (*re-cor-dare*, to give back to the heart). Like the Prodigal Son who, "when he came to himself" (Luke 15:17), remembered that his home was with the Father, we need to remember and to "come to ourselves." We need to remember the deepest and often unconscious desires of our heart. We have to relearn how to see with the eyes of the heart in order to become aware of the invisible reality of God's Love that is actively present in and among us. The exile of forgetfulness of God — the land of alienation, isolation, and imprisonment in self-centered concerns — has many faces. They become visible and conscious when we dare to live in the polarity of tensions, when we "come to ourselves." Coming home to God and to ourselves entails a willingness to live consciously in the tension between the alienations and conditionings that hide our own true identity so effectively and the fiery light of God's Love, which pursues us passionately to bring us into its presence.

The remembering (*recordatio*) Hildegard speaks about consists of a certain consciousness of God's loving presence rather than of the remembrance of specific information about God. Our bounded, limited, conditioned, fearful, and measurable world becomes radiant with potential in the light of this remembering:

> But you, O human being, possess the remembrance [*recordationem*] of good and evil; it is as if you were standing at a crossroad. (SC I, 4, 30)

> Whenever hatred tries to darken my being, I raise my eyes to the mercy and martyrdom of the Son of God and thus tame this desire. In faithful remembrance [*fideli recordatione*], I breathe the fragrance of roses which spring from the thorns. In that way I recognize my Redeemer. (SC I, 4, 7)

> Only faith can fathom the overflowing Love that surpasses all understanding: that God redeemed the human through the Incarnation of his Son. (WM I, 4)

As I mentioned earlier, Hildegard's most often used symbolic narrative for the journey out of alienation is the parable of the Prodigal Son. She interprets it on three levels: the relationship of human beings to God, to creation, and to the cosmic reality. The archetypal image that speaks most sharply to the necessary attitude for the first step on the journey home is the "Fear of the Lord" (SC I, 1). This figure is all eyes to the God-reality. Symbolic images like the Fear of the Lord, which we met in an earlier chapter, have the power to connect the limited realm of bounded perception with the energy of Divine Love and the depth of human yearning. Symbols, archetypal images, and the mythic stories of Scripture provide personal and communal patterns for the journey home to God, which is also the journey into fuller humanity. Our age is less used to the power of symbolic thinking than Hildegard's monastic culture was. When the Rule of St. Benedict, for instance, speaks about "the light that comes from God" (RB, prologue 9), a medieval reader would immediately make the connection that this phrase connotes the light of God that comes through Scripture. This symbolic connection does not happen as easily for modern readers. As a specific perception of truth, a symbolic phrase bears many layers of meaning and provides insight for the self in relationship to God, to society, to tradition, to history, and to the cosmos. Grounding the person in a common cosmos of meaning, a symbol invites participation. This focus is important because Hildegard's writings abound with symbolic language that only reveals its richness when we let it resonate on many levels.

The act of remembering that Hildegard describes as the first step on the "way of the heart" has both a subjective component and an objective content. The subjective experience is a graced gifting that is available to everyone. The Good News is the objective content that helps Christians to bring their subjective experience to its intended communal fullness within a framework of meaning. The subjective experience in the act of remembering is an awareness of living in the exile of forgetfulness and also an awareness of a deep desire to return home; it is a remembering that we need God's grace to become truly creative. The objective component of the act of remembering is not a definite doctrinal articulation but rather a "sensing" of the true law of God in the depth of the heart, in the depth of Scripture, and in the depth of history; it is an experience of an eternal truth seen as in a mirror darkly. Hildegard tells us that it is a remembering of Christ and also of "our Mother Zion" in the depth of the heart. The term "Mother Zion" points to God's motherly care of which the soul becomes conscious at the same time that it becomes conscious of its captivity. It is felt as an inner stirring that had been dormant. It can lead to a contemplative knowledge of the heart that "knows" the motherly care of Divine Wisdom and desires to come home. A heart hardened by fear can now become softened by the life-giving waters of grace and wake up to the reality that home, the Kingdom, is right here, in and among us, that the journey home to God starts in the cave of the heart.

In vision I, 4 of *Scivias*, Hildegard illustrates this journey home, the way of the heart (see illumination 5, p. 89, above). As the embodied soul returns, by God's grace, from error to Zion, her true homeland, she laments:

> Where am I? In the shadow of death. On what path do I travel? On the path of error. What consolation do I have? The consolation of a pilgrim in exile.... When I remember you, O Mother Zion, in whom I was meant to dwell, I see the bitter slavery to which I am subject. And when I remember all the strains of music that sound in you, I became aware of my

wounds. When I remember the delight and joy of your glory, then I detest the poisons that pollute them....If I would not know you now, then my pain would be easier to bear. I flee now from my evil companions because wicked Babylon has put me on a leaden scale and is bludgeoning me with heavy beams so that I can hardly breathe. But when I sigh in tears and groans, O my mother, then wicked Babylon sends forth such noise of roaring waters that you cannot hear my voice. Terribly upset, I will look for narrow paths on which to escape from evil companions and my unhappy captivity. (SC I, 4, 2)

Second Step: Groaning in Sorrow

A groaning in sorrow (*gemitus recordationis*) arises simultaneously with the remembering I have tried to describe. Painful awareness of sinful patterns of forgetfulness of God and of our true identity is mingled with deep desire. Pains of powerlessness and deep remorse are mingled with pains of love and desire. Desire for God's presence is mingled with awareness of our absence. Without this specific sorrow, these sighs of body and soul, we are not in touch with God, Hildegard tells us. These sighs act like healing medication. Much of contemporary sensitivity and spirituality tends to repress or project pain and sorrow. We have lost an awareness of this important dimension of the spiritual life, as Caecilia Bonn, OSB, has pointed out (see *Weg zu Gott: Hildegard von Bingen-Lehrmeisterin des geistlichen Lebens*). Sighs (*suspirium*) and groans (*gemitus*) of the spirit embrace all the emotional, imaginal, and intellectual powers of the psyche. They are experiences of integration, experiences of joining our sorrows to those of God, who can redeem and transform them into new forms of love and creativity:

The soul goes about in earthly affairs, laboring through many changes just as the earthly condition requires. But the spirit raises itself in two ways: when it is filled with sighs, groans and desire for God, and when, so to speak, it seeks discernment concerning power, control or desires for a variety of things; for it knows how to discern rationally. The human being contains a likeness to heaven and earth. (SC II, 1, 2)

Sighs and groans of sorrow and desire lead the way home; they shake up the illusion of security and become an inner dynamic. Many of our spiritual mothers and fathers throughout the centuries knew about the healing power of tears and of groaning in sorrow. Hildegard reminds us that every event in salvation history was preceded by the groans of God's people. The Son was sent because of the groanings of God's people. He embraced his destiny with sighs and groans (Heb. 5:7). Mary groaned when she said: "I am the handmaid of the Lord, let it be done to me according to your will" (SC II, 6, 15). St. Paul tells us that "all of creation groans as in childbirth waiting for the sons and daughters of God to be revealed" (Rom. 8:19). With the help of the Holy Spirit, we are impelled to groan inwardly with remorse and remembrance (Rom. 8:22–26). God meets us where we are most wounded, in the very place we so long avoided and evaded. Sighs of desire for heaven, as Hildegard calls them, are the work of the Holy Spirit in us: "Grant me, O Lord, through your power the fiery gift that will extinguish the ardor of perversity in me, so that I might drink with proper sighs [*rectis suspiriis*] from the waters of the living fountain which grants me joy of life" (SC III, 10, 7).

Groaning in sighs and sorrow not only will lead to a greater awareness of God but will also reconnect us with the depth of our emotional and spiritual capacities. In a way it is remedial work that is needed to heal any overreliance on information and the intellect as sole sources for resulting actions. The affective way of the heart, however, encourages an integration of the entire spectrum of genuine emotional capacity with the rational approaches we are capable of. Hildegard, using biblical imagery, tells us that only the heart is capable of "cooking" the powers of our soul with the Word of God as revealed in Scripture and history into "life-giving food." The power of God's fiery Love needs the kindling of our deep sighs. In our sighs, as Caecilia Bonn reminds us, we touch the heart of God. But Hildegard is aware that we tend to avoid the route of letting sighs and groans rise from the depth of our being, that we need God's help.

The church — according to Hildegard — grows in holiness through the profundity of sighs offered on the hidden altars of faithful hearts. As burnt offerings of the heart, these sighs and groans are the way in which we meet God. The fire is the fire of our desire for God in which these sighs are transformed — or, as Hildegard would say it, "cooked" — into the food of life and love. This becomes quite explicit in the "Son of Man Speech":

> From your conscience I seek the wounds and pains of your heart....Behold, I look at you. What are you meant to do? Whenever you call out to me in this labor of conscience, with wounded heart, eyes moistened by tears, shaken by fear of my judgment, and when you persevere in crying out to me to hasten to help you,...then I will do all you desire and I will make my dwelling place in you. (SC III, 10, 3)

God is experienced not only as life-giving light but also as a God of awesome demands and fiery zeal who confronts and empowers us on this way of the heart. When remembrance (*recordatio*) and groaning in sorrow (*gemitus recordationis*) have opened up a human being, then genuine freedom of the heart becomes possible, freedom to cooperate with God for and in this world. Whenever the way of cooperation with God is not chosen, an alternative way to God opens up, the way of repentance. For Hildegard, repentance is a world-renewing force, the strong power of life and love of God that was set free in the Passion of the Son. Hildegard expands our often anemic understanding of repentance by making it a manifestation of our potential to know and live true interrelatedness with even the elements in the cosmic body of Christ. She advises people who at the hour of death can find no priest to stand before the air to confess their sins, for they have polluted her! A softening and a deepening of the heart are preparation for the third step on the road home: good works done in and with God.

Third Step: Good Works in and with God
(*Opus bonum, opus Dei*)

The first two steps on the way of the heart have opened the human being, made the person receptive to the creative energies of God (*virtutes*) that flow from the heart of God and enfold the human being in the womb of God's motherly care. Good works, done in and with God, are possible because in Christ all powers of God became fully relational and manifest. They continue to empower us. The divine energies of God become incarnate in the universe if — with converted, repentant, and discerning hearts — human beings bring good and just works to birth. This is what Hildegard calls the work of God (*opus Dei*). Benedictine monasticism used the term *opus Dei* to refer to the praise of God through the chanting of the Divine Office. Hildegard retains this contemplative focus but greatly expands it. The term now includes all good works a person performs for and in God. They are the work of God and, at the same time, the work of the person through whom Christ's presence bears fruit in action.

In *Scivias*, Hildegard shows us that to walk the way of faith, hope, and love we need to live out of the powers of God she calls *virtutes*. The powers, or energies, of God that Hildegard treats extensively in this book are those of her Benedictine roots: Fear of the Lord, Poverty of Spirit, Humility, Obedience, Chastity, Wisdom, and Discernment. A later book on ethics takes her insights into the human spirit and psyche and its potentials and pathologies beyond the monastic context. We meet thirty-five powers of God and the vices that oppose them. If we embrace the task of incarnating these powers of God, then they can guide us into decisive choices as we join the long historical caravan of pilgrims who travel the way of the heart (*iter cordis*) in hope:

> "Listen! I am standing at the door, knocking; if you hear my voice and open the door I will come to you and eat with you, and you with me" (Rev. 3:20). That is to say: you, who faithfully love your Redeemer, see how I wait for you at the tent of your heart, waiting to help you. I know what your conscience beholds in the exploration of your heart, and I shake up your spirit with gusty winds of memory, so that it opens itself to goodwill. When the believing heart hears the voice of the Fear of the Lord, then I unite myself with it, embrace it, and enjoy unfailing food with it, since it offers me a marvelous taste, the taste of itself in its good works. Therefore this heart shall have the food of life in me, because it loves what brings life to those who desire justice. (SC I, 2, 25)

The transformative journey Hildegard describes as the way of the heart, the *iter cordis*, is a variation and expansion of the Benedictine journey: "Clothed then with faith and the performance of good works, let us set out on this way, with the Gospel as our guide, that we may deserve to see him who has called us to his kingdom" (RB, prologue 21).

In Hildegard's description of the journey of the soul and her desire to return to Mother Zion, the soul finally overcomes her enemies and travels on the narrow path with the help of the "wings of her soul" — the divine energies or powers — until she reaches a tent "whose interior was made of strong steel": "I entered and from now on I did works of the Light where I had previously done works of darkness. I built...and built... and built" (SC I, 4, 3). Attacked by her enemies while she built the tent, the soul now laughs at them and says:

> The Master who built this tent was stronger and wiser than you....I have fought painful and difficult battles against you as you tried to put me to death; but you could not. Protected by strongest armor and brandishing sharp swords, I defended myself against you. Retreat, retreat therefore. I am no longer yours. (SC I, 4, 3)

Hildegard would sternly admonish anyone who speaks about knowing or experiencing God without any resulting involvement in the world. Her test for the authenticity of these experiences are good works done in and with God. Good works as the work of God, the *opus Dei*, are the fruit of transformed, purified, and discerning heart-consciousness. In contemporary terms one could say that action arising from the contemplative journey of the heart becomes the link between the implicate, enfolding, Trinitarian order of the universe and the explicate, unfolding order of human potential in the realm of time and history. The embodied soul needs to become the womb-tent in which the Mystery of God can grow and be born into the world, into the great womb where the inner life of God, the great Trinitarian dance of ever-living Light and Love, wants to become present.

Chapter 7

Life in the Tension of Opposites

And when you are able to discern the just and the unjust roads, then I will question you: "Which road do you wish to travel on?" (SC I, 4, 30)

In the reality of life we find ourselves continually at the "crossroads of decision," according to Hildegard of Bingen. Either we can make choices for God, for goodness, for our true self, and for interrelatedness in this world, or we can respond to the draw and power of all opposing inclinations and powers. These choices are not easy. In order to make them, we first need to claim all the particulars we encounter in our consciousness as our own — the good, the bad, the illusory, the real, the wounded, the healed. These encounters are a way of coming into a living relationship with the Mystery of God. Only then will we become sources of creative choice and action in a broken, wounded world.

Hildegard urges us to cultivate the God-given power of discerning these choices, to not hide in unlived life, and to have the courage for the difficult but ultimately life-giving choices we can make when we consent to live at the still-point in the tensions we encounter in life. We live in many fields of tension: body and soul, men and women, God and human, heaven and earth, action and contemplation, compassion and justice, creation and redemption, humility and self-worth, life and death, historical conflicts and desire for God, to name just a few.

The human and Christian task, Hildegard tells us, is to live in the implicit and creative tension of both poles. "The crossroads of decision," the still-point in the tensions of life, is the portal into the fullness of a life where we become words who make present the fecundity of the Word that came forth from the Mystery of God. The "way of God" is the way of living creatively at these still-points in the field of historical tension. "The way of darkness" leads to the destruction of any life-giving, creative tension of polarities. Hildegard tells us that God created us in such a way that discernment of the two ways and of the many polarities of tension these ways represent is both a birthright and a task:

> You, O human, have the remembrance of good and evil — you stand at a crossroads, so to speak. If you despise the darkness of evil and desire to look up to him whose creature you are, . . . then consider how you have been taught to turn away from evil and do good and that the heavenly Father did not spare his own Son but sent him for your deliverance. And pray to God to help you! Hearing you he will say, "These eyes are pleasing to me!" If you then cast off weariness and run courageously within God's commands, God will hear the cry of your supplications. . . .
>
> I say to you, if God is good, why do you put such little value on knowing his goodness in which he handed his Son over to you, the Son who in many labors and sorrows delivered you from death? When you say that you cannot do good works, you speak in wicked injustice. For you have eyes for seeing, ears for hearing, a heart for pondering, hands for working, and feet for walking, so that your entire body enables you to stand up and lie down, sleep and wake, eat and fast. Thus God created you. . . .
>
> Therefore, O human, if you turn your eyes to the two roads, that is to good and evil, you learn to distinguish things great and small. How? Through faith you recognize the one God in his divinity and humanity; and in evil you see the works of the Evil One. And when you are able to discern the just and the unjust roads, then I will question you: "Which road do you wish to travel on?" If you wish to travel the good paths and faithfully hear my words, then persist in sincere prayer, asking God to come to your aid and not to abandon you, for your flesh is weak. Bowing your head in hu-

mility quickly shake off and cast away all that is evil in your works....

But you, O human, are blind when you need to see, deaf when you need to hear, and foolish when you need to defend yourself because you consider God's gift of discernment and the five senses of your body as no more than filth and futility. Do you not have understanding and discernment? The Kingdom of God can be acquired, but not in trifling ways. (SC I, 4, 30)

Hildegard's prophetic challenge was to speak about the ways of God, to wake people up to an awareness that they must stand at the crossroads of the two ways that meet in the depth of every heart in its encounter with the reality of life. Any "awakening of the heart," as it is called in Scripture, results in a greater consciousness of God's presence. Walls of fear and conditioning can crumble and reveal new potential in the light of that presence. Hildegard challenges us, as well as her contemporaries, to live securely at the still-point in the tension of opposites we encounter at the "crossroads of decision" in our heart. She challenges us to treasure the gift of discernment God gave us and tells us that God-forgetfulness reigns in the hearts of all those people who trust more in themselves than in God. It reigns in the hearts of those who are asleep to the choices that — in Christ — are a human birthright and task. Hildegard calls us out of the defended realm of God-forgetfulness into an awareness that conflicting motivations can become conscious, can become the very place where discernment of life-giving or life-inhibiting choices takes place.

Contemporary spiritual wisdom might use different terms to refer to the reality Hildegard's calls "the crossroads of the two ways." We might call it discernment, growth in transparency, transformed perception, or truth experienced in sacred space where reality resisted our plans and alienated us from safe but constricting categories of thinking and living. As people on a spiritual journey — who sense the reality of the Divine Mystery — enter those spaces, they usually discover a deep desire for God and also an incredibly complex mixture of their motives. They discover a mixture of presence to God and of deep-seated resistance to it, a mixture of love of God and protective self-love, a mixture of an inborn deep desire to be fully relational in God's image and the internalized "shoulds" of parents and other authorities whose approval they have learned to crave. Yet they might also discover that all of life is a supreme gift and that all the movements of their hearts, be they exuberance or withdrawal, ecstasy or feelings of abandonment and despair, need to be housed in their hearts as rhythms of the loving mystery that pervades all there is. What Hildegard calls God-forgetfulness (*oblivio Dei*) opposes the spiritual journey; it withers the rhythms of life and love. It often justifies itself in words like these: "How can we know anything about a God we have never seen? And why should we pay attention to something that we have never met?" (MV IV, 67).

In the twelfth century Hildegard focused on a fact that contemporary consciousness research in a variety of fields is quite aware of: our motivations and emotions are evaluative judgments about something; they are a way of "seeing" and "acting" through the lens of our own experience. Religious experience is an integral part of this. We need to learn to distinguish between the lenses of conditioned, fear-filled, and injured experience and the lens of contemplative experience, the lens of profound desire to let Love happen. Hildegard's terminology and method are historically and culturally conditioned and need to be translated into the language of our day. When Hildegard asks us to carefully listen to a dialogue of opposing "voices" that takes place in the human heart, her language might well resonate with the stirrings of our own hearts. Do the focus and particular mode of expression of a twelfth-century visionary theologian hold any truth for contemporary society or modern God-seekers? Do Hildegard's insights into the depths of conflicting motivations and emotions that reign in the human heart transcend the specific consciousness of her time? Does her message hold transcultural truths that need translation for men and women of the twentieth century? I think so.

What, specifically, are some modern manifestations of the God-forgetfulness Hildegard speaks about? Our culture surrounds us with the siren call of self-reliance, with illusions that everything in this world is intelligible, that we can be in charge of almost everything. Contemporary spiritual gurus promise that we can change ourselves into prosperous, healthy, and well-adjusted people. The question of God is left to the churches, to theologians, to the experts in this specialized field of inquiry. The question of motivations and emotions is left to experts in ethics or psychology. Focus on the "I" overshadows needed connectedness as "we." Social responsibility and moral integrity are eroding. Violence, depression, addictions, and lust for power run rampant in personal as well as in social and global relationships, while fear of the "stranger" increases.

We are easily drawn into the conditioning and norms for conformity set by our culture. In addition we develop our own norms and preconceived values, which are most often unconscious. We develop emotional substitutes for our deepest needs, substitutes that stem from emotional needs of childhood that were never met, substitutes that can grow into demands and "shoulds" for others. A variety of personally tailored substitutes strive to protect the "injured" self, which has never known unconditional love or genuine relatedness. The struggle to let these unconscious motivations become conscious under the guidance of the Holy Spirit is a "spiritual path." As we travel it, we meet the false, conditioned self and move toward the freedom of knowing ourselves as the beloved of God, the freedom to live life in the tensions of opposites. Our age is quite aware of the causes for many of the personal and social pathologies that lead into unconscious conformity, but rarely do we discover a prescribed therapy that is as profound and all-encompassing as Hildegard's interrelational spirituality.

Hildegard tells us that human beings are meant to be nestled into community with nature and history like the branches of a tree, not in theory, but with their bodies, emotions, relationships, and discerning actions. She speaks about the existential dialogue that takes place in human striving for relatedness to the self, to others, to nature, and to history as being our dialogue with the living God. It is opposed by all forms of grasping to preserve well-known but constricted forms of life. This is the "crossroads of the two ways" she speaks about. We are not meant to focus only on ourselves, Hildegard advises. Every aspect of our being in this world is meant to be relational in a cosmos and historical context where everything is interdependent. As a matter of fact, fear-driven self-reliance leads to aridity and the exile of God-forgetfulness, which, she reminds us, manifests itself in unrelatedness.

Hildegard does not tell us who God is but rather that God is. Like the Greek Fathers of the Church, Hildegard speaks about energies of life, light, and healing that pour from the heart of God. She calls them "virtues." They oppose the powers of darkness and chaos she calls "faults" or "vices." In her theological framework, God's therapeutic powers or energies are gifts of grace that need human receptivity and cooperation to become incarnate in responsible choices in history. Set free in Christ, these energies and powers inhabit, surround, and enable human beings to become co-creators. They are spiritual energies that help in reconnecting body and soul, man and woman, individual and society, heaven and earth, God and human beings. They entice, enable, and support our consent to embrace the sufferings and joys that living life in a creative field of tension entails. If we choose to open ourselves to these powers, we become capable of entering the moment of *kairos*, the sacred space of the present moment. From that space we can make decisions rooted in the bright-burning understanding (*rationalitas*) that waits to be born from the depth of heart and mind. From that space we can make choices for life. Cooperation with the opposing powers of darkness leads to an aridity of body, soul, and relatedness, which is manifested in the drive for power, in violence, or in depressive life-aversion.

Hildegard invites us to wake up from the many forms of anesthesia that comfortable and defensive patterns of thinking, feeling, and interaction represent. She asks us to open our eyes, hearts, and emotions to the conflicting motives that reign in our hearts. She asks us to wake up to the reality that we often embrace only one pole of tension or even avoid all tensions of life. Yet she assures us that the Living Light will illuminate any darkness and fear we find as an "exile of God-forgetfulness"; she assures us that the divine energies will help us to willingly sacrifice our narrow, injured consciousness whenever we trust God and put our experiences in dialogue with the great journey of Christ through history. In Hildegard's Trinitarian framework, the powers and energies of God become present, active, and vivifying in this world whenever human beings are willing to enter the birthing process of becoming more fully incarnate, more fully conscious, more interrelational. According to this perspective, enduring the labor pains of the "new creation" means joining the great journey of Christ through history. It means to willingly stand at the crossroads of decision, it means to willingly embrace the crucifixion of the conditioned, fear-filled, God-forgetful self.

The Dialogue of the Heart

How to live life at the crossroads, in the tension of opposites between the powers of God and the powers of darkness and God-forgetfulness, is the theme of Hildegard's ethical work, *Liber vitae meritorum* (The Book of Life's Merits). A visionary work, it does not argue ethical problems abstractly but rather offers a symbolic image, the dialogue between the vices and virtues that takes place in the human heart. In chapter 4, we met the visionary figure of a man so tall that he reaches from the rim of the sky to the depth of the abyss. In this visionary image the cosmos is the realm of action for the triune God, the Cosmic Man of this image, from whose breath a fiery cloud filled with life-giving powers, the virtues, emerges. In *Liber vitae meritorum*, we meet thirty-five personified virtues; they confront thirty-five personified vices, powers of the rebellious spirit that opposes God and tempts human beings to not believe in a God whom they can neither understand nor see.

A lively dialogue between personified vices and virtues invites readers then and now to face our particular situation and to decide for or against relatedness in the historical arena. Hildegard must have met the latent potential for cooperation with or rejection of the powers of God in herself, in her sisters, and in people she met — otherwise she could not have given such accurate descriptions of the motivation of the human heart. In what follows I give some examples of the dialogue between opposing motivations. Although Hildegard's language and imagery seem unusual to modern men and women, readers might still discover an accuracy and sharpness of discernment in these dialogues that translate well into the movements of the heart in contemporary society.

"Hardened Heart"/"Compassion"

"Hardened Heart" [*Obduratio*] speaks:
    I did not create anything and did not give life to anybody. Why should I go through the trouble of caring for anyone? I will support people only to the degree that is advantageous to me. God, who created everything, should take responsibility for the universe and care for it! What good would it do to speak up or get involved in the affairs of others?...For if I always have pity on others so that I do not get any peace, what is left for myself? What kind of life would I have if I responded to all voices of joy or grief? I only know about my own existence! (MV I, 16)

"Compassion" [*Misericordia*] answers:
    Oh you petrified being, what do you claim there? Plants offer each other the fragrance of their blossoms; each stone shines its brilliance on the others; and every creature instinctively desires the loving embrace. All of creation is of service to human beings, and in this service of love she joyously gives her goods to them. But you, you are not even worthy to have a human shape!...But I live in the air and in the dew and in all of greening freshness like a delightful healing herb. My heart is full and willing to help anyone. I was present in the beginning when God said "Let there be," and creation, which now is of service to humankind, emerged....With loving eyes I consider all essential needs and feel related to everything. I raise up all whose spirit is broken, I am a salve for every pain. (MV I, 17)

Hildegard has her ear on the pulse of life, on the struggle that takes place in the human heart, on the profound desire to mirror the God-reality. Even a frozen, petrified human heart that is ruled by self-absorbed, egocentric concerns is capable of opening up, of responding with compassion. It is still capable of true empathy that joins it to others in a life-giving interrelatedness, Hildegard tells us. It still has the capacity to join in the flow of life-giving fiery Love that is meant to suffuse all there is. To stand securely and trustingly in the center of tensions is not easy, but it is truly life-giving.

"God-Forgetfulness"/"Holiness"

"God-Forgetfulness" [*Oblivio Dei*] speaks:

Why should I not follow my own ways when God does not care for me and nothing about God is ever felt by me? I want to pay attention to whatever is profitable for me and do whatever I want to do. Whatever I know, understand and like, that I want to do. (MV IV, 8)

How often we hear variations of this attitude in our day and age! How much of our culture is focused on success, power, enjoyment, and a trust in human knowledge and desires that totally denies the subtle movements of God's life-giving presence among us!

"Holiness" [*Sanctitas*] answers:

...What are you saying? Who created you, who called you to life? God alone! Why can't you see that you did not create yourself? I, I call out to God and ask for everything that is needed for life. I live in harmony with God's plans and remain there by seeing and recognizing God. How does that happen? Through a good conscience I quickly become present. With it I sense God, and... I pluck the zither of prayer by adoring and knowing God with it. If I... paid attention [only to my own selfish needs], I would... turn away from God. For it is not the earth which provides human beings with food, clothing, and other things they need, but God himself. Human beings observe that everything grows, but where this originates and how it happens, that they do not see. (MV IV, 9)

Hildegard's repeated advice to flee from God-forgetfulness and to return to God is not a call to move into a spiritualized avoidance of involvement with this world. Any movement of our heart toward the living God, who is present in all of history and creation, is a movement toward the world, which is meant to flourish in the peace of relatedness; it is a movement into the historical field of tension.

"Cowardice"/"Power of God's Victory"

"Cowardice" [*Ignavia*] speaks:

I strive not to harm anybody, for if I did, it might result in a lack of consolation and help for myself. If I harmed some-

one, I might possibly risk my own existence and enjoyment.
I will rather flatter the rich and famous. I need not concern
myself with the saints and the poor, because they are of no
help to me. I will try to please everyone in order not to become a loser. If I disagreed with people, I would certainly
be defeated. And if I wronged them even a little, I would
receive a greater wrong in return. As long as I live among
people, I want to live in peace with them. If they act right
or wrong, I will keep quiet. I gain more through occasional
lies or deception than through speaking of truth. It is better to take than to give, better to evade the mighty than to
block their way.... In any case, I own the little house I selected for myself. Those who speak the truth often lose all
their possessions, and those who take up the battle perish.
(MV I, 19)

Not to harm anybody is a good trait, one could say, but Hildegard unmasks the deeper implications of cowardice. To not ever
take a stand, to be ever tolerant because of self-protection, is a
shriveling up of our relational potential; it is a refusal to root
ourselves in reality; it is a refusal to root ourselves in God; it is
a refusal to live in the tensions of life.

The "Power of God's Victory" [*Divina Victoria*] answers:
    ...In your unsteadiness you not only walked — shaking
and callously — into your own exile, but you also deceived
other human beings with the fickleness of your kindness.
You lack the right criterion for judgment.... Whatever you
desire and attract to yourself is petty and insignificant non-
sense. I myself do not desire a life that is located in ashes,
and I do not desire futile emptiness. I rather yearn to reach
the overflowing fountain. Therefore I take up the battle...
and will stay in the truth of God. (MV I, 20)

To become who we are meant to be requires the courage to
leave the spaces of hiding and self-protection and to stand at
the crossroads of decision, Hildegard advises. It requires a rising consciousness of having lived in fear-filled neutrality that
evaded decisions and involvement. She describes this movement as a battle in the depth of the human heart between
opposing motivations. Spirited and spirit-filled argumentation

is necessary so that the truth of God can become incarnate in the world. We only discover who we truly are if we make these inner decisions for God in the concrete circumstances of life, if we enter the arena of radical obedience to God, in whose image and likeness we are made. Without the powers and energies that come out of the heart of God we cannot enter, fight, or win this battle.

In these days of more creation-centered spirituality, Hildegard's terms for these two motivations could be seen as a dualistic distinction. If, however, we carefully listen to the words of these personified motivations, we might discover that the same ambivalence Hildegard illustrates for twelfth-century readers still reigns in contemporary spiritual yearnings.

"Love of the World"/"Love of Heaven"

"Love of the World" [*Amor saeculi*] speaks:
Why should I shrivel up? After all, I brim with greening fecundity. Should I drag along like an old man while blooming in the freshness of youth? Should I be blind to the lovely light of the eyes? I should blush with shame if I acted thus. As long as I can still enjoy the beauty of this world, I shall blissfully embrace it. I do not know another life, and the tales I hear about it do not mean anything to me. (MV I, 10)

There is nothing wrong with living life to the fullest. It only becomes problematic if that is all there is. Hildegard points out that the attitude of loving the world becomes problematic when life's meaning and purpose are restricted to this enjoyment only, when the deep human desire for God is not acknowledged and cultivated, when only one pole of the tension is stressed.

"Love of Heaven" [*Amor caelestis*] answers:
You are not looking for genuine life, which never shrivels in its freshness of youth and does not exhaust itself even in the maturity of old age. You lack all light! You stumble in the darkness of night and bury like a worm into human desires. You live from moment to moment and then dry up like hay....
I, however, am a column of divine harmonies, and all joy of life is my concern. I do not scorn true life! (MV I, 11)

What Hildegard names "Love of Heaven" is really a profound love of this world. This kind of love does not enjoy or devour creation and life for its own pleasure but rather finds traces of God and challenges of grace in the fullness of relatedness it desires.

"Rage"/"Patience"

"Rage" [*Ira*] speaks:

I crush everything and destroy anything that gets in my way. Should I tolerate what I see as injustice done to me? What you do not want done to you, you should not do to me. I fight with my sword and hit with clubs when someone wants to harm me. (MV I, 22)

The power of rage is a blinding force, is unaware of the tension of polarities in which the balance of life is found. Closely related to cowardice, it crushes anything in its way.

"Patience" [*Patientia*] answers:

I am the gentle breeze in the life-force of fecundity. I cause the blooms and fruits of virtues to sprout and then erect a secure lodge for them in the hearts of people. Whatever I begin, I finish; my loyalty is unceasing and I do not annihilate anyone. (MV I, 23)

Life in the balance, life lived in the tension of polarities, becomes possible if we open ourselves to the powers and energies of God, the virtues, while — at the same time — recognizing the powers that oppose them. If we are honest, we recognize that most often we are at least partially asleep to life in the creative polarities of tension. Our desires and our stance toward others, creation, and history are not too different from those of Hildegard's contemporaries. But our historical context and contemporary consciousness are very different. They produce very specific patterns of absolutized autonomy and elicit specific patterns of response and avoidance.

Depression seems to have been no stranger to Hildegard. She accurately describes the feelings of weariness and pessimism in the life of a depressed person. I assume that the following dialogue refers not to what we nowadays call a clinical depression but rather to people who tend to slide into melancholy moods and hopelessness yet are still capable of responding to the beauty of nature or to life in its many forms.

"Weariness of Life"/"Heavenly Joy"

"Weariness of Life" [*Tristitia saeculi*] speaks:

Woe to me that I was born! Woe! What good is life? Who will help me, who will save me? If God cared about me, such suffering would not happen. It does not help to trust God.... If he did something good for me, then I would have proof for God's existence. But I don't even know what I myself am. Created for misery and born in misery, I vegetate without any consolation. What good is life without any joy? And why do I live in this world where nothing good will happen for me? (MV V, 15)

"Heavenly Joy" [*Coeleste Gaudium*] answers:

You don't know what you are saying.... Look up at the sun and the moon and the stars, contemplate the glory of fecundity in creation, and consider just once how with all these God gave human beings such blessings.... If the day approaches, you call it night! If good fortune knocks at your door, you call it a curse. And when everything goes well, you insist that it does not....

I already possess heaven on earth, because I look at everything God created from the right perspective, while you only speak about despicable matters. I tenderly take the blooms of roses and lilies and all of fecundity [*viriditas*] into my heart by singing praises of all of God's works, while you pile pain upon pain upon God's works. In all you do you act so forlorn.... I do not do this. I dedicate all my activities to my God. Joy is the other side of sadness. (MV V, 16, 17)

The energy of fecundity (*viriditas*) cannot find a home in a heart that is filled with pessimism, bitterness, or narcissism; it cannot find a home in self-protective structures. *Viriditas*, the healing, relational energy of God who is Love, needs a partner, needs to become incarnate in Wisdom. Fecundity is the work of Christ, according to Hildegard. Human beings have a role in the creative, relational process. Self-centered isolation short-circuits any cooperation with the creative powers of God. What we deeply desire, Hildegard tells us, is to become who we can be, mirrors of God. In and through us, God is victorious against the powers of evil if — in obedience — we stand at the "crossroads of decision" and discern the way of God in faith. We will have to live consciously in the tension of opposites; we will have to discern — with others — the way of peace. Our hearts, minds, and bodies have to become conduits through which the therapeutic powers of the Living Light touch creation and history. This kind of "awakening of the heart" has personal, psychological, communal, political, and ecological dimensions:

> For Wisdom displays the work of her glory in good people. But where did they come from, these works done in righteous justice, which adorn the Heavenly Jerusalem? From the height of heaven. For just as from the heavens the dew comes down and waters the earth with its moisture, so do good works come down from God and are moistened by the dew of the Holy Spirit so that a person of faith might bring forth good sweet fruit and become a citizen in the heavenly city. Thus the divine works, which come down from heaven on human beings through the gift of the Holy Spirit, do contain the glory of God from whom they issued. (SC III, 10, 31)

Discernment

> O, you foolish people, lukewarm and shameless, you wither away! You don't want to open even one eye to see what you really are in the integrity of your spirit.... You act as if you had no understanding of good and evil, nor the honor to know how to avoid evil and to do good. (SC III, 10, 1)

This is the beginning of the "Son of Man Speech" in *Scivias*, a speech that lists many manifestations of human brokenness. The speech is an invitation to all human beings, not only to believers, to wake up and to recognize their key position in the cosmos, history, and salvation history. It is an invitation to become aware of the crossroads of decision where our key position as co-workers with God becomes incarnate. The desire to know who and what we are meant to be is at the core of our existence:

This is how your creator builds. He gave you a most precious treasure, namely a vibrant understanding, for he greatly delights in you, his creation. He instructed you through the law he instituted, to use this very understanding to bring profit in good works and to be rich in virtue, so that through this the good giver of gifts would be more accurately known. You must therefore contemplate always in which way the great gift you received — to be used for others, as well as for yourself in works of justice — should bring forth in you the brilliance of holiness, so that people, called forth by your example, give honor and praise to God because of it. If you multiply it profitably in all justice, then praise and acts of thanksgiving will stretch toward a knowledge of God who has inflamed these virtues in you through the power of the Holy Spirit. He will turn to you in the compassion of his grace and through the sweetness of his delight he will set you aflame in a firestorm of love for him. Filled with the consolation of the Holy Spirit you will wisely discern all that is good and you will do even greater works. Burning with love you will glorify your Father who has kindly granted this to you.

May my sheep hear these words, and whoever has the ears of the interior spirit heed them! For it pleases me that people who know and love me should be busy in such a way that — affected by the gifts of the Holy Spirit — they interiorly understand how to act. (SC III, 10, 9)

One of the powers or gifts of this firestorm of love is discernment, an interior understanding of what is good or evil and of how to act. It is the fruit of a transformed, purified, repentant consciousness that has been gained on the way of the heart (*iter cordis*). Discernment is more than the following of a moral law, more than ethical choices, more than rational or emotional choices for what we commonly perceive as good. The grace of God effects it in and with human beings (SC III, 2, 10):

> Charity rising
> from the vast abyss
> past the stars above
> abounds in all worlds,
> unbounded love,

> and with spousal kiss
> disarms the sky-king. (SY 141)

Grace — or to use another Hildegardian phrase, "the fire-storm of love" — is composed of many powers or energies of God that are available to us. It surrounds human beings like the loving arms of a mother, consoling, encouraging, protecting, confronting, and pushing them into the reality of life. Hildegard personifies many of these energies she calls virtues. One of them is *Discretio* (discernment). In one of her visions, *Discretio* speaks the following words:

> I, the mother of virtues, observe the justice of God in all things. For in spiritual battle and in the tumult of this world I always wait upon God in my consciousness. I do not condemn, I do not trample, I do not despise kings and dukes, leaders and other secular office-holders in the historical order established by the creator of all things. Should it be permissible for ashes to spurn ashes? The crucified Son of God turns to everyone exhorting them according to his justice and mercy. (SC III, 6, 7)

Hildegard reminds us that to be responsible in history, human beings need discernment. She invites us to find the "crossroads of the two ways" where discernment, a movement of the heart and mind that is initiated by Christ, becomes possible. In Hildegard's theological/spiritual framework, discernment (*Discretio*) is one of the creative, therapeutic energies or powers of God that are available to us if we freely choose the way of God. Like healing remedies, these powers can restore health to an ailing and alienated person. Only then — with God, with each other, and within an interdependent earth community — can people creatively imagine a therapy for breaking the cycles of violence, fear, and oppression.

Discernment is neither easy nor without the pitfalls of deception. A discernment process ponders and evaluates choices, motivations, actions, and consequences. It differs radically from problem solving by rooting the process in the Mystery of God that permeates the entire historical context. It involves the conviction that a focusing of heart, mind, and will might lead to a still-point where the abiding presence of God will become conscious in a particular situation. We most often need others to listen with us for the guidance of the Holy Spirit; we need others to listen with us for deceptions, evasions, or movements in trust within a specific situation.

The Christian tradition has always been aware that we need to test the spirits in order to see if they are from God or from the powers of darkness. It advises that we look at the fruits. Over the centuries, a real science of discernment evolved that has its roots mostly in the mystical tradition. Hildegard's writings on discernment add new facets to this rich tradition. She herself must have slowly learned the difficult art of balancing all involvements, interactions, and deeds in the spirit of discernment. Her own standing at the crossroads of decision had its source and motivating power in the depth of her being, where she came to know herself as deeply loved and challenged, as part of a universe that is meant to be interrelated in a symphony of praise and mutual support. The ancient theme of "the two ways" resonated so deeply with her that it became a major image in her writings.

Hildegard's symbolic, poetic images are a language of transition that can shed new light on a traditional theme, making discernment and resulting action an act of love for and in creation and history. True symbols evoke associative, analogical thinking. They amplify and point to connections that can heal personal states of alienation. They also connect this newly healed subjective experience of meaning to that of the larger community. Contemporary studies have shown how the symbolic/mythic level of perception functions as the connecting link between sensory, psychological/historical consciousness and the consciousness of spiritual or ultimate reality. Therefore, symbolic thinking and symbolic images, as a language of transition, play an important part in the process of discernment. If Hildegard's symbolic universe resonates with our own search for meaning, then this language of transition is doing its work.

The term "discernment" comes from the Latin *discernere*. It means to clearly distinguish or differentiate things that are not alike and to hold them in due proportion. In a Christian understanding, the proportion or norm is Jesus Christ. Discernment (*Discretio*) thus becomes the gift of discovering and evaluating different motivations of reacting to reality according to their source and effect. According to Hildegard, discernment is the foundation and mainstay of a spiritual life, of a life of genuine relational fecundity. It has a double focus, inward toward identity and outward toward discerning involvement. It also has a double context, the unseen reality of God's presence here and now and the specifics of our moment in history. For Hildegard, discernment means deciding according to God-intended proportion, not according to what "feels" comfortable when one selects among possible choices or what seems to best fit present circumstances. Discernment seeks an attitude of wise moderation, of balance. Hildegard indicates that the gift of discernment does not deal with general norms, but it is given by God according to the specific strengths and weaknesses, according to the specific psychic wounds and defense mechanisms, of the individual or a community. An opening for the reception of this gift happens when people awaken to their deep desire for God's way and simultaneously become conscious of their attraction to, or cooperation with, the opposing powers. Hildegard tells us that the way of God leads to awe, reverence, and a desire to bring all that is separated, split off, or alienated into an interdependence that mirrors the Trinitarian mystery. The way of Lucifer, the *diabolos* (Gr.: the one who throws apart, thwarts, disintegrates), strengthens the protective walls of fear, separation, and alienation that prevent this mirroring and genuine fecundity in history. The distinguishing power to discern (*discretio rationis*), a focused and balanced awareness, becomes possible when we wake up to the choices at the crossroads of the two ways.

Hildegard, a Benedictine, was naturally influenced by the Rule of St. Benedict that governed her life. The Rule advises that the abbot, specifically, as leader of the community, needs the wisdom of discernment. He needs the wisdom to know when to encourage and when to rebuke. He is the one who is called to the right balance, to right moderation in interaction with the community. He is the one who is called to always "let mercy triumph over judgment":

> Excitable, anxious, extreme, obstinate, jealous, or over suspicious he must not be. Such a man is never at rest. Instead he

must show forethought and consideration in his orders, and whether the task he assigns concerns God or the world, he should be discerning and moderate bearing in mind the discretion of holy Jacob who said: "If I drive my flocks too hard they will all die in a single day" (Gen. 33:13). Therefore drawing on this and other examples of discretion, the mother of virtues, he must so arrange everything that the strong have something to yearn for and the weak nothing to run from. (RB 64:16–20)

Few of us are abbots. But the wisdom of Benedict's advice holds for all who are called to leadership in a community, be it family, the business world, charitable organizations, or politics.

Hildegard's Benedictine understanding of discernment has to do with the right balance, with a balance that resonates with God's way, with the Word of God in Scripture, with the Word's abiding presence in history and creation. It has to do with the core desires of our humanity, with a profound awareness of the needs and abilities of others. It is not easy to reach that balance. We search for it hesitantly and with uncertainty. We look for it in the voices of authority old and new, in people, in groups, in books, in churches, in social institutions, and in new communities. It is not easy precisely because this right balance is much more than the human ability to distinguish with the intellect. It has to with doing the will of God for us; it has to do with encountering the cleansing, life-giving fire of the Holy Spirit; it has to do with courage and wisdom. Courage and wisdom are required to discern the origin and direction of feelings and desires from which our commitments to action flow so that we may move with greater clarity in the direction of active fecundity, of *viriditas*. Whatever wants to grow and bear fruit must be able to bear up under a spirit of discernment that has its source in the fecundity of God and is oriented by the pattern of the Gospel. To "see" the heart of another or to "see" the heart of a contemporary problem is not easy. Our own hearts, which are meant to do the discerning, are filled with all kinds of attachments and desires. They are so filled with business and concerns that they are most often weary and unavailable. In addition, the constant danger of deceit is very real. Why should we even bother? Hildegard urges us not to take this one-sided view but to enter into the tension of opposites. She would admonish us to learn that discernment is the task of the spiritual life.

She offers us a wide array of metaphors and images to tell us about this attitude of balance, of discernment. We meet *Discretio* imaged as "opened eyes," "gossamer web of rays," "cross-bearer," "light-receiver," "light," "fruitfulness, " "firmament," "mother of virtues," "merchant," and "the cornerstone." All these images point to Divine Wisdom, who is waiting for us in the marketplace, offering the power of discernment. Every image also points to the human task to receive *Discretio,* this power or energy of God, in order to gain the wisdom of deciding and acting justly.

In the first visions of *Scivias,* "Fear of the Lord," a strange archetypal figure totally covered with opened eyes, points to an attitude that is needed to make discernment possible. Before her stands the figure of a child, "Poverty of Spirit," whose head is totally immersed in a stream of light flowing from a book (a Gospel) on the lap of a shining Christ figure. In the shadow of his protective wings she follows the traces of the Son of God. Both figures, symbolic images of needed attitudes, are surrounded by a shower of glowing sparks, the powers or energies of God. "Fear of the Lord"

> shrouds herself in the penetrating vision of good and just intention and effects eagerness and steadfastness in human beings. Because of all the opened eyes you cannot even see a human shape. With the sharp blade of her vision she chases away all forgetfulness of divine justice which human beings often experience in the weariness of their heart. (SC I, 1, 2)

"Fear of the Lord," a stance of awe, represents both gifts of God and a necessary human attitude to become present to the Kingdom-reality. "Poverty of Spirit" points to a necessary emptying of all that is false, fear-filled, and falsely self-protective. Living in this spirit will lead to a sharpened, penetrating sensitivity that knows that the Kingdom-reality has its source in Christ, who always was and is and will be. "Fear of the Lord," a figure that is all opened eyes, awake to reality, functions as a symbol that provides a reference point for our deep yearnings as human beings. It points beyond our individual lives into ever deeper and wider levels of truth on the level of participation in the experience of the God-reality in all of creation and throughout history.

The same symbol of "opened eyes," or vision, is used in Hildegard's letters, where it speaks to the choice, to the ability, and to the task of faith-filled discernment. She accused Bishop Daniel of Prague of having "vision too dull to see where discernment lies, that discernment which wisdom produced," and told him to "rise up and to look into the sun [of Christ] with due moderation" (L 107). In a letter to Pope Eugenius, she encouraged him to clean his eyes, to become discerning:

> He who knows and discerns all creatures, Who rouses them and is watchful over them, the Living Eye sees and says: the valleys are complaining against the mountain and the mountains are falling on the valley. What does this mean? Subordinates are no longer disciplined by the fear of God.... Purify your eyes so that nothing escapes your notice. Let your mind be watered by the pure fountain so that you may shine with the sun and imitate the Lamb. (L 36–37)

Being awake to the Living Light, to the Love that pervades all, enables discernment. It is never an easy task. Like Wisdom, discernment is one of the powers of God that will not be opposed when it is rooted in *rationalitas*, the bright-burning understanding that is rooted in Love: "Just as the power of God encompasses and pervades all things and cannot be opposed by any obstacle, so too human bright-burning understanding [*rationalitas*] has the great power to resound in living voices and to rouse sluggish souls to wakefulness with a melody" (SC III, 13, 13).

A precise ordering of things in "a gossamer web of rays" illuminates another facet of discernment. The "web of rays" image comes from the great vision in Hildegard's cosmological work where she "sees" the entire cosmos and the human being in its center as an organ in the womb of God that is embraced by the blood-red, fiery circle of Love, the Cosmic Christ (see illumination 4, p. 80, above). The human being stands cruciform in the center, moving an intricate web of rays, which are connected to the elements and the stars, to the cosmos and history, like a net:

> And finally you see that a light that is brighter than the clearest day emerges like a gossamer net from the mouth of the described figure in whose breast the cosmic wheel appears. From the primordial source of real Love, in whom the cosmic order rests, shines her exceedingly precise ordering of all things. It comes to light in ever new ways, holding and tending everything there is. (DW II, 46)

This "exceedingly precise ordering of all things" is the very pattern discernment tries to discover and live. It has its source in the heart of God, in the movement of Love that measures, orders, and tends everything in a balanced but ever-new way, Hildegard tells us. Human beings are meant to discern and mirror this ordered balance in their lives. Genuine discernment is, however, a "rare bird," in the words of Richard of St. Victor. We tend to overemphasize one side. We are attracted to either action or contemplation, to either the human or the Divine Mystery, to either old ways of consciousness or escape into illusory liberations. What is difficult for us is to stand in the center of tensions of what we perceive as polarities; what is difficult for us is to become the very person in whom these polarities are interrelated, in balance; what is difficult for us is to discern the counterforces to the incarnational movement made explicit in Christ; what is difficult for us is the balance between sense perception, emotions, insight, and action. We waver between overconfidence and desperation, between body and spirit, between absence and presence to this movement from the heart of God that pervades all of reality. Yet we are meant to become its presence — we are called to make Christ present in the cold stable of our world. Our soul is capable of standing in the tension, Hildegard consoles us. The God-given power of discernment will balance the specific powers of our soul, she tells us. It will balance the ordering and weighing, the bright-burning understanding and the emotions. In contemporary Jungian terminology, we might say that this God-given energy entices the gradual unification and integration of the elements of consciousness (i.e., cognitive awareness, affect, sensation, and imagination), that it is a manifestation of the Self, the potential incarnated wholeness of a person.

The very image of how discernment becomes incarnate is the Crucified One, the totally obedient one, the one who is the cornerstone of the building of salvation in history. The unfathomable Love of God, which became manifest in the utter vulnerability of the child in the manger, in the man on the cross, and in Mary, wants to become incarnate in our vulnerability. Only a life lived on the wings of faith will let us perceive this profound truth of our faith. To live in such vulnerability seems impossible and totally unreasonable to fear-filled, protective, and conditioned ways of perception. It just demands too much. Grace, the firestorm of love, needs to smooth the way until unrestricted energy can unite the realm of God with the realm of this world through discerning choices of human beings. The gift and task of discernment enable us to distinguish more clearly between love for its own purpose and genuine creative love. It enables us to distinguish more clearly between imposed justice of our own making and justice that is a manifestation of God's love.

In Jesus, the Christ, the energy of discernment became visible and tangible, according to Hildegard of Bingen. In the Holy Spirit it continues to enflame, surround, and encourage us. The entire cosmic and historical order is meant to manifest the choices for interrelatedness made at the "crossroads of decision" in repentant and hope-filled human hearts. We need compassion and repentance, great remedies offered by God, to come in touch with the needs and sufferings of this world and with the hardness of our own hearts. We need these to grow in discerning sensitivity.

Hildegard's visionary images often point to a felt tension of absence and presence, ours and God's, as the pathway into the creative historical tensions of our lives. Her images speak so powerfully of God's ever-present Love that they can resonate with a felt absence of that reality in our own awareness. They can, however, also strengthen our own small awareness of that presence. A few examples of symbolic images of *Discretio* that refer to this felt tension may help clarify these points.

In *Scivias* (III, 6) we find the figure of *Discretio* sitting at the end of a wall in the building of salvation, which is slowly rising in history. She rests on the cornerstone, which represents Christ. On the shoulder of this figure appears a huge cross on which is the image of the Crucified One. It moves back and forth, indicating that her task is done in the spirit of the Son, that her task is in relation to the Love of God, which became fully manifest in the Crucified One. A stream of brilliant light comes out of a cloud. It represents God's mercy, which inflames and illuminates human hearts with the gift of wise discernment. It refracts into her chest and abdomen, signifying the distinct and specific gifts of the Holy Spirit, which can enter the human heart through the slits that represent humility: "The Holy Spirit pours these rays, more brilliant than the sun and incredibly discrete into humble vessels, namely the sharp-sighted eyes of the soul of believers, thus illuminating their senses and hearts so that in all circumstances they precisely discern appropriate action in God" (SC III, 6, 34).

In her right hand *Discretio* holds a small wooden fan. With the help of the Holy Spirit she considers her works "on the wood of fragile flesh," and with the help of God she "drives away the flies," the devil's temptations. The top of the fan blossoms, indicating that faith in a Trinitarian God enables the power of discernment. All kinds of small gemstones rest in the lap of this figure. She sorts them carefully and diligently, like a merchant who looks over his wares:

> This is to say that in the core of the heart she holds in the gemstones of the virtues all that is apt and suitable in the most minute plans and practices. Cautiously and diligently she scrutinizes for God-ordained justice so that in all things she might appropriately and justly lead the way in human hearts. (SC III, 6, 34)

Mary, the woman impregnated with the presence of God, emerges in Hildegard's writings as the incarnation of *Discretio.* The balanced attitude of discernment became manifest in her willingness to live in the tensions of life with an openness to God, to her deep self, and to the realities of her world.

Hildegard's insight into the gift, power, and task of discernment gives us glimpses into the realm of *viriditas,* the realm where what is of this earth and what is of God are no longer separate. She invites us into this realm where we become aware that everything in creation has a spiritual component, where we become aware that genuine spirituality needs to be lived in the creative tensions of life on earth and in history. Hildegard knew this invisible, spiritual component of all of reality so profoundly that she created a kaleidoscope of images that point to this reality and to the human task to take our place in the interrelated order of our world. Her images can help us to evoke and strengthen awareness of this realm in the reality of our lives.

As we become aware of this realm of *viriditas,* the realm of genuine fecundity, we come to know what it means to stand at the crossroads of decision. We gradually learn to distinguish between a deep pain that arises from the depth of a heart impregnated by God, a pain that brings us into solidarity with all the sufferings of this world, and the pains that do not arise from this deep source. I am talking about pains that have their source in the conditioned, wounded self — pains such as feelings of rejection, inadequacy, and fear. These conditioned pains have a way of paralyzing the true self, which wants to come to know itself as loved and cared for, as the place where Wisdom wants to set up her tent.

We must come to discern two ways that lie within each of us: the road of fear and the road of love. Each has a multitude of manifestations. In the personal struggle of discernment, which precedes discernment of the two ways in the world around us, we can come to the way of God through an ongoing struggle with false or conditioned pains. If we get in touch with the mechanisms of the road of fear, we can reach the still-point of discernment, where we come to know the fears we experience as the survival mechanisms we developed in response to the wounding of our lives. If we come to see this, then the truth of the road of love is already being mirrored in our recognition of how we distort the present experience, how we deceive ourselves, and why we needed to do it. What is being mirrored is a manifestation of the firestorm of love, of grace, which penetrates through every crack of our hardened, defended, and fearful hearts to heal us. The way of God, the way of living in the creative tensions of the here-and-now, will reveal the real pains that the birthing of our true identity as a child of God in an interrelated universe entails. It is the way of faith, hope, and love.

Chapter 8

Building Wisdom's House in History

> Sophia!
> you of the whirling wings,
> circling encompassing
> energy of God:
>
> you quicken the world in your clasp.
>
> One wing soars in heaven
> one wing sweeps the earth
> and the third flies all around us.
>
> Praise to Sophia!
> Let all the earth praise her! (SY 101)

The "way of God," the way of our true humanity, requires relatedness to both God and people for its development; it requires relatedness to the transcendent and to the immanent. Our contemporary world is often silent about the hunger of the human heart for God; it is also silent about our hunger for experiences of interrelatedness that reveal the footprints of Divine Wisdom's presence in history. Hildegard speaks eloquently to this hunger, seeing its source in God's hunger or need to be in a relationship of mutuality and fecundity with us. People can become the delightful, dazzling, green garment of Wisdom in history, Hildegard points out, through the graced fecundity (*viriditas*) of their works and good intentions:

> God's works are so secured by enveloping plenitude, that no created thing is imperfect. It lacks nothing in its nature, but rather possess in itself the fullness of all perfection and

utility. And so all things which came forth from Wisdom, live in her like a most pure and splendid adornment, shining forth with the most splendid radiance of their individual essence. When fulfilling the precepts of God's commandments, people, too, are the delightful and dazzling garment of Wisdom. They serve as her green garment through good intentions and the living fecundity of works adorned with virtues of many kinds. (WM IX, 2)

Becoming Wisdom's green garment is rooted in the mystery of the Word. He was with the Father from the beginning, became incarnate, and continues to permeate all spheres of reality: creation, the human community, divinity itself, and also eternity and time as the mystery of the Cosmic Christ:

> You, all-accomplishing
> Word of the Father,
> are the light of primordial
> daybreak over the spheres.
> You, the foreknowing
> mind of divinity,
> foresaw all your works
> as you willed them,
> your prescience hidden
> in the heart of your power,
> your power like a wheel around the world,
> whose circling never began
> and never slides to an end. (SY 259)

Wisdom/Love/*viriditas* emerged out of the eternal counsel of God, shone forth in the Incarnation of the Son, and continues to shine forth in history through discerning good works of people as Christ, the Wisdom of God, gathers them and all of creation to himself:

For from the beginning of the world — when Wisdom first openly displayed her work — a straight path, adorned with holy and just commands, extended to the end of time. It was first established through the greening sprouts of patriarchs and prophets who in their affliction and wretched lamentation sighed with great desire for the Incarnation of the

> Son of God. Then she was graced with the dazzling virgin-
> ity of the Virgin Mary; next with the solid and ruddy faith of
> the martyrs; and finally with the brilliant and light-filled love
> of contemplation, by which God and neighbor ought to be
> loved through the heat of the Holy Spirit. (SC III, 9, 25)

The mystery of the Incarnation is central to Hildegard's visionary symbolic theology. Hildegard grounds both the feminine mode of receiving, incarnating, and housing divine fecundity (*viriditas*) and the entire Paschal Mystery in the core mystery of the Incarnation. It reveals how God and this world are brought into intimate relationship. It reveals a mutuality of grace and human response as *viriditas*, and its absence as the betrayal of this potential, as aridity. Wisdom's house in history is built when Sophia, the "circling encompassing energy of God," finds a home in our hearts, intentions, and deeds.

God-centered lives of prayer, adoration, and the interior authority of graced discernment are the concrete places where Divine Wisdom leads us out of the morass of self-centered motivations and into the accountability of responsible choices in an interdependent world, Hildegard tells us. Good works have their source in the power of divine mutuality and fecundity (*viriditas*), which seeks expression in and through us. When we respond to the empowering energies of God in faith and hope, we become living building stones in the house Wisdom builds in history. We become a functioning part of an organically interrelated universe and living words of praise:

> To the Trinity be praise!
>   God is music, God is life
>   that nurtures every creature in its kind.
> Our God is the song of the angel throng
>   and the splendor of secret ways
>   hid from all humankind,
> But God our life is the life of all. (SY 143)

When we step out of the realm of God-forgetfulness and begin to walk "the way of God" in praise and the inner dialogue of discerning choices, we become part of the Incarnation, which — according to Hildegard — is not a one-time event only. It is the eternal process of divine fecundity becoming incarnate in time and space in the needy and fragile vessels of particular humble and repentant human hearts:

> For this is why human beings have discernment of good and evil, that they themselves in all their works may know God better by avoiding evil and doing good....
>
> O unfortunate people, who refuse to know the great glory of being made in God's likeness! (SC III, 8, 8)

> The radiance of God shines in the good works of just people; in them God is ever more ardently adored and worshipped on earth. And through these virtues the holy city becomes distinctly adorned. For human beings worship God in countless deeds of wonder when — with the help of God — they perform good deeds. (SC III, 10, 31)

> Speak, reveal the bread which the Son of God is! He is life in fiery Love. He rouses from sleep all who are dead in body or spirit. He dissolves sins into bright splendor, he who is himself the rising life of holiness in us. (SC III, 1)

> Through the fountain-fullness of the Word came the embrace of God's maternal love which nourishes us into life, is our help in perils, and — as a most profound and gentle love — opens us for repentance. (SC II, 2, 4)

Hildegard knew the divine heartbeat and the maternal embrace of God so well that she dared to be God's prophet in word and action. Inviting us to meet Christ as the Wisdom of God who "pervades and penetrates all things" (Wis. 7:23), she calls us into a spirituality that unites action and contemplation. She does not call for a slavish imitation of her particular transformation in God or of her specific involvement in the affairs of her time. Her spirituality and symbolic theology can encourage contemporary God-seekers to experience transformation in God through experiences of grace, supported by the cosmos of meaning she draws with the grand sweep of her symbolic images. Hildegard calls the spiritual journey simply "the way of God." It is the way into interrelated mutuality, into the fecundity of *viriditas*. In Hildegard's spirituality the personal journey is not antithetical to collective, social, and political concerns. Both are integral to the Christian vision of Christ's long journey through history as Wisdom incarnate. Hildegard tells us that we assume our responsibility in the great cosmic drama between God, human beings, creation, and history whenever we recognize the arid wastes of our God-forgetfulness and open ourselves to repentance and the gift of God's healing energies. This process starts in a feminine mode of receptivity in our particular lives as men or women.

Only dialogue in a spirit of collaboration and discernment will enable us to embrace our unique historical roles as humans on our planet. Hildegard's symbolic images, which draw the grand design of God's abiding presence, can support the emerging consciousness of this graced and difficult task. The Christian symbolic universe she draws for us makes the historical responsibilities we face at the dawn of the twenty-first century a "spiritual" task. To become part of the communal journey of an interrelated earth community we need to become — in Hildegard's words — "all opened eyes"; we must learn to listen with the "ears of the heart." To live in hope, while creatively envisioning a world beyond current patterns of isolation and destitution, requires a breaking out of confining or stereotypical patterns of thought, language, and action. It requires that we do not hide from or deny the true facts of the present situation. It requires that we become discerning and bold enough to discover hidden agendas, our own and those of our culture and communities. It requires us to stay open to new invitations of grace. It requires constant dialogue. This is a sobering and frightening task. The great Christian framework of meaning Hildegard draws can support these efforts. It can help us not to lose heart when we leave behind secure ways of knowing and being to enter the darkness of an unknowing that can serve as the womb for the fecundity of the Living Light.

The great attention our culture pays to individual growth, coupled with an emphasis on the spiritual journey as a personal one, has left many of us unprepared for the depth of cultural blindness and for the systems that sustain it. It prevents us from pursuing the communal task of building a community of peace and justice as a spiritual task. Hildegard would probably point out that any spiritual journey takes place in a social, cultural, and religious context. "Seeking God" in an existential dialogue with history and creation — supported by a life of prayer, by the wisdom of the Scripture, and by our personal and communal dialogue of discernment — is the "sacred remedy" Hildegard advises for the God-forgetfulness of isolated, self-protective lives. In our present context, the "sacred remedy" for the ecological devastation we experience might take the form of a dialogue with the entire earth community into which we are nestled. Human communities, not only individuals, are capable of becoming willing, discerning conduits for God's therapeutic energies. When we cooperate with them, these divine energies can break up the arid destitution of our own creation.

Hildegard challenges us from across the centuries to consider the communal journey and communal discernment as a spiritual process. It might take us to "crossroads of decision" where the fecundity of Christ, the Wisdom of God — if it is called by that name or not — leads entire communities through repentance into the breakup of old securities and ever-new forms of fecundity.

The "Heavenly Jerusalem": Symbol of Faith and Hope

In Hildegard's writings, the "Heavenly Jerusalem" functions as a symbol for the spiritual process of building the Kingdom-reality:

> Then I saw a new heaven and a new earth; for the first heaven and the first earth had passed away and the sea was no more. And I saw the holy city, the new Jerusalem, coming down out of heaven from God, prepared as a bride adorned for her husband. And I heard a loud voice from the throne saying, "See the home of God is among mortals. He will dwell with them as their God; they will be his peoples and God himself will be with them; he will wipe every tear from their eyes." (Rev. 21:2- 4)

As contemporary Christians face the tasks and challenges of becoming a globally interrelated earth community, radical faith, hope, and compassion need to arise from wise discernment and profound repentance so that new shapes and challenges of the Kingdom-reality can be perceived and worked for. The Heavenly Jerusalem is not only a reality at the end of history: it is now, Hildegard tells us. It refers to the Kingdom that is meant to be here "on earth as it is in heaven":

> So then you are no longer strangers and aliens, but you are citizens with the saints and also members of the household of God, built upon the foundation of the apostles and prophets with Jesus Christ himself as the cornerstone. In him the whole structure is joined together and grows into a holy temple in the Lord, in whom you also are built together spiritually as a dwelling place for God. (Eph. 2:19-22)

> Therefore, I took secret counsel with myself to send my Son for the redemption of humankind, so that humans would be brought back to the Heavenly Jerusalem. No iniquity could withstand this counsel. For when my Son came into the world he gathered unto himself all those who, forsaking sin, wanted to hear and imitate him. (SC I, 2, 15)

> O Jerusalem, founded
> on glowing stones, shooting
> stars, sheep lost and found:
> Christ called and publicans raced,
> sinners made haste
> to your walls to be laid in place.
> (SY 195, stanza 7)

Few people in our age live as totally immersed into the coded stories and symbols of Scripture as Hildegard did. In her monastic culture the "Heavenly Jerusalem" was a scriptural theme that suffused liturgy, prayer, and consciousness. It spoke to the task of her life: the search for God. Hildegard's often unlettered contemporaries were also exposed to the theme's symbolic power. The Romanesque architecture of their churches and cloisters invited them into a sacred cosmos, to which this image points. In Scripture and tradition, the Heavenly Jerusalem theme does not function as a prediction of the physical destiny of the human race on earth, although it has often been used in this way. It rather refers to the spiritual building process of a city, a community, which not only is from on high but is "already and not yet" gradually built up on earth in faith and hope.

For Hildegard this hope was founded in the abiding presence of the Word-made-flesh that revealed the maternal wisdom and love of God as the bright-burning understanding that desires *viriditas*, interrelated fecundity. We are all called and capable of becoming part of this building process. The bright-burning understanding of Love needs to find a home in and among us:

> Bright-burning understanding is the matrix of the knowledge of good and evil; it functions like a builder who erects and tears down. Whoever loves the daylight of faith builds his house in the Heavenly Jerusalem; whoever detests it, wrenches his house away from the honor and radiance of the heavenly inheritance. (WM V, 25)

Does the Heavenly Jerusalem symbol have any relevance for believers today? Can it still invite us to become part of the history whose culmination is in God? Can it still give rise to thought and shape to the present, or is it a biblical symbol that does not touch the consciousness of contemporary searchers? These are questions that need to be asked. Each of us must listen and see if Hildegard's communal symbol connects our own experience and desire for God with the unseen historical reality to which it points. We must see if Hildegard can invite us into the depth dimension of the here-and-now when she describes the Heavenly Jerusalem as a spiritual building process that takes place in the entire sweep of history, revealing an ever-greater connectedness with the web of life and the Mystery of God.

The Heavenly Jerusalem symbol, like all of Hildegard's symbolic images, requires a way of seeing "with eyes that see the inner things," eyes that are learning to chart both the personal and also the social and communal dimensions in the topography of the spiritual journey. In the "Son of Man Speech," Hildegard calls this way of seeing a Spirit-gifted vision. It refers to a spirituality that does not escape from reality but rather views all of reality "with eyes that see the inner things":

> And thus the works of the Spirit are shown to the faithful and holy soul just as the Heavenly Jerusalem is to be built spiritually..., by Spirit-gifted labor. The greatness and loftiness of works done in the Holy Spirit become manifest in the

measure by which the city is adorned with the good works performed by people touched by the Holy Spirit. Thus set on a mountain it consists of countless buildings. She assembles the most precious stones in herself, the holy souls in the vision of peace, purified from the decay of sin. And so with these precious stones it will shine like gold, for Wisdom displays the brilliance of her work in good people. But where did they come from, these works performed in proper justice, which adorn the Heavenly Jerusalem? Obviously from the heights of heaven. Just as the dew descends from the clouds and sprinkles the earth with its moisture, so do good deeds descend into humans and are watered by the rain of the Holy Spirit so that the person of faith might bring forth good sweet fruit and become a citizen in the heavenly city.... The glory of God shines in the good works of the just so that on earth God is ever more passionately sought, adored, and honored. (SC III, 10, 31)

Our participation in the spiritual building process — which has very concrete manifestations depending on the historical context and its challenges — was intended by God before all ages, Hildegard tells us.

Her world is not ours. In the twelfth century, Christendom was the world Hildegard knew. Every facet of society was part of it. The contemporary world is very different. Christianity no longer suffuses society, culture, and politics. Contemporary mentality is as culturally and historically conditioned as Hildegard's was in the twelfth century. Is there, however, a transcultural message in the Heavenly Jerusalem symbol that survives translation into contemporary language and context? Let us follow Hildegard's thread of developing the biblical symbol and see if it holds implications for our age.

Hildegard draws a grand design of the "building of salvation," which is slowly but incessantly rising. Christ is its cornerstone, connecting the beginning and the end of his mystical body in history. Hildegard never tires of praising Mary, who in her life received and incarnated the divine fecundity when she was overshadowed by God. The Word's intended Incarnation became possible through the fecundity of Mary. In the "Antiphon for the Virgin," cited earlier, Hildegard expresses how Mary's fecundity was a manifestation of God's eternal fecundity, how her maternity brought forth the restoration of the entire created universe. Mary became the "matrix of light," revealing a face of Wisdom:

> Resplendent jewel and unclouded brightness
> of the sunlight streaming through you,
> know that the sun is a fountain leaping
> from the father's heart,
> his all-fashioning word.
> He spoke and the primal matrix
> teemed with things unnumbered —
> but Eve unsettled them all.
>
> To you the father spoke again
> but this time
> the word uttered was a man
> in your body.
> Matrix of light! through you he breathed forth
> all that is good,
> as in the primal matrix he formed
> all that has life. (SY 115)

Another face of Wisdom, of God's eternal fecundity as the ongoing work of Christ, is revealed in the church. Hildegard depicts the church as the corporate entity in which the net of Christ is thrown wide so that she might gather all who are called to become God's co-workers. Following a difficult course through history, she is continually assaulted by exterior and interior forces, especially in the last days when the Antichrist will arise in the very womb of the church (SC III, 11). In *Scivias* (II, 6), Hildegard symbolizes the church as the golden figure of a woman who emerged out of the eternal counsel of God and was given to Christ as his bride when he hung on the cross. She received baptismal rebirth and the Eucharist as wedding gifts so that all might become — through him and in her motherly care — partakers of the Trinitarian life of Love. After offering that symbol, Hildegard never again imaged the church as being already fully present in history. Only her torso is shown when Hildegard refers to the historical reality.

In Hildegard's spiritual architecture each individual believer, as well as the church as the community of believers, is meant to become the earth in whom God — in the Word and through the Holy Spirit — plants seeds of that selfsame fecundity of Love that is the Trinitarian nature. If we house it, she tells us, we become active, Spirit-gifted building stones in the final communal reality, which is slowly rising in history with Christ as the cornerstone.

Hildegard fused the biblical symbol of constructing the Heavenly Jerusalem with her understanding of *viriditas* as the Christic fecundity of interrelatedness permeating the whole of human existence, history, and the cosmos. When God's way and the human potential for response intersect as fecundity (*viriditas*), she tells us, then we already experience a foretaste of a future fullness of the presence of God:

> "And I saw the holy city, the new Jerusalem, coming down out of heaven from God, beautiful as a bride prepared to meet her husband" (Rev. 21, 2). This signifies the following: The bride signifies the holy and adorned soul who is betrothed to Christ through the dowry of his blood. She looks at him like a bride at her bridegroom. For the Son of God descended into the womb of the virgin out of which he erected the new and holy Jerusalem. The angels who incessantly look at the face of God, look with wonder at the works of the holy ones. (WM IV, 87)

If the Heavenly Jerusalem symbol connects our own experience in any way with a communal Christian cosmos of meaning and the web of life to which the symbol points, then specific tasks arise from this awakening. Profound sorrow of repentance can arise if God-forgetfulness and aridity of dissociation from the greater environment are really felt. That sorrow can rekindle the part of ourselves where we know with the bright-burning understanding of Love that we only live justly if we regain a sharpened sensitivity for our responsibility for this earth and each other. This is the God-ordained order and our task. Hildegard never tires of pointing out that it is a spiritual task to assume our unique role as humans within an organically interrelated universe and in history, for "everything that exists in the order of God responds to the other."

Chapter 9

Love
(*Caritas*)

ANTIPHON FOR DIVINE LOVE

Charity rising
from the vast abyss
past the stars above
abounds in all worlds,
unbounded love,
and with a spousal kiss
disarms the sky-king. (SY 141)

Our unique spiritual role as human beings within an organically interrelated universe has its source in the mystery of Divine Love (*Caritas*), which transcends and enfolds all. Experiences of presence and absence, or *viriditas* and *ariditas*, mediate the mystery of this Love, which penetrates all with the mutuality of interrelatedness. Love is the matrix or womb in which we live and grow and have our being:

Love [*Caritas*] speaks:
"During the day and at night I cause the virtue of balance and of good deeds. Day and night I spread my cloak. I cause good deeds during the day and at night I anoint all wounds; not the slightest reproach can be brought against me. I am the amiable friend at the throne of God, and God hides no decisions from me. The bridal chamber of the king is mine, and all that is God's is also mine. Wherever the Son of God wipes out the sins of human beings with His Garment, there I bandage the wounds with softest linen." (MV III, 8)

The air with her sharp powers signifies faith who is a banner of victory. Like the air that shines in a fiery flame, so does faith indicate the right way and the dew of hope which moistens the spirit of believers. Because they sigh with heavenly desire, they posses the fruitful freshness of perfect love and hasten to be of help to others. Therefore they can bring forth their supplications with tears, moved by the breath of repentance, just as a mild breeze brings forth blooms. In their desire for heaven they thus bear richest fruit, the food of life so to speak, for their own use and for the use of many others. (MV 6, 22)

To gain access to Hildegard's difficult and historically conditioned texts it is helpful to focus on some of the key symbols and archetypal images of the grand cosmos of meaning she weaves for us. As we have seen, they can create bridges between our personal story and the ineffable experience of God, between our experiences and the story of the human community as part of the web of nature and history. They are, in fact, one way to bridge the centuries between Hildegard and us.

The Matrix of Creation, Redemption, and Bright-Burning Understanding

In Hildegard's symbolic framework of meaning, God's Love (*Caritas*) is the matrix from which all of creation emerged. Wisdom, who desires to build her house in history, has her source in this Love. Christ, crucified and risen, the Wisdom of God, is the manifestation, goal, and moving power of this Love in a universe that is meant to be an interrelated, Trinitarian energy pattern of Love. Love opposes evil and suffering. Human beings participate in this pattern of mutuality and interrelated fecundity (*viriditas*), which — in the Holy Spirit — is the work of the Son. They are called to embody it in the midst of their own struggles in a world that abounds with self-protective isolation. Opposing this aridity are good deeds — discerned through bright-burning understanding in love (*rationalitas*) — that find their origin and cause in that same matrix, Love. In other words, connectedness in mutual interrelatedness is at the heart of reality as it is meant to be. To bring the new creation about, we — and all of creation — groan in the pains of childbirth.

The symbolic images of Love in Hildegard's visionary framework speak to the "taste of mystery"; they invite us on a difficult but blessed journey into our concealed reality, which has its source in the Divine Love. Hildegard's many symbolic images of Divine Love reveal different facets and modes of this reality, which is the source, cause, and motivating power of our journey. She gives us a whole bundle of meanings, which together point to the paradoxical experiences of this hidden reality at the center of life.

It is important to see Hildegard's symbols not as a step to clearer conceptual articulation but rather as a specific way of doing theology and mystagogy. Hildegard does not describe what is but rather points to something that is not yet fully present here and now. Hildegard's language, which we might experience as imprecise, delights in ambiguity and paradox and through this very mode participates in the gestation of Divine Love in the womb of our being. It points to forms of being and consciousness that do not yet exist and simultaneously calls into question the way things are done and perceived. If, however, we merely read her symbolic language as a descriptive account of Hildegard's own experiences, then this language loses its power to call us into the creative fecundity and mutuality to which all of Hildegard's symbols point.

Symbols respond to the deep need to bring to light the most hidden dimensions of what it means to be a human being made in the image of this Love and called to live its presence on this earth and within a particular historical community. Symbols reveal a universal truth; they contain a deep coding for the personal and collective journey; they give meaning to epiphanies of grace, to human resistance to this reality, and to hope. Let us revisit some of these symbols to tie our explorations together. The "way of God" turns out to be the "way of Love."

In Chapter 3 we saw how in *Scivias*, Hildegard imaged the Love of God that she experienced as a shining Christ figure (see illumination 1, p. 52, above) enfolding the Kingdom-reality with wings of boundless justice. The human attitude before the Mystery of God, whom she experienced as the Living Light, is awe, "fear of the Lord." Later visions sharpened Hildegard's God-image and her understanding of Divine Love. The Love she continued to experience as the Living Light became more explicit as the incarnate Word of God and as the fecundity of Love that is at work in the entire universe. In *De operatione Dei* (The Book of Divine Works), this Love is imaged as a magnificent winged figure whose face is ablaze in clarity (see illumination 2, p. 56, above). When Love (*Caritas*) speaks, she reveals herself as the matrix and primal force of life for all of creation and also as bright-burning understanding:

> "I, the highest and fiery power, have kindled every living spark and have breathed out nothing that can die. But I determine how things are — I have regulated the circuit of the heavens by flying around its revolving track with my upper wings — that is to say, with Wisdom. But I am also the fiery light of divine essence — I flame above the beauty of the fields; I shine in the waters; in the sun, the moon, and the stars I burn. And by means of the airy wind, I stir everything into quickness with a certain invisible life which sustains all." (WM I, 2)

> Just as the power of God encompasses and pervades all things and cannot be opposed by any obstacle, so too human bright-burning understanding has the great power to resound in living voices and rouse sluggish souls to wakefulness. (SC III, 13, 13)

Hildegard used the unusual Latin term *rationalitas* rather than *ratio* for reason or understanding. I have translated this term as "bright-burning understanding in love" because it refers not to reflexive consciousness but rather to an experience of being part of this Love, part of a mystery too vast to put into rational categories. Human beings are capable of bright-burning understanding in love, Hildegard tells us, because we are made in the image of God, who is the fountain-fullness of the bright-burning understanding.

The choice of the term *rationalitas* also reveals the influence of Hildegard's Benedictine spirituality and monastic culture — the second bridge I suggested as helpful for crossing the gap of the centuries. This bright-burning understanding is a kind of savoring with the spiritual senses that is meant to lead from repentance to freedom, awe, and the fertility of interrelatedness rather than to intellectual clarification only. It is an ability gained in "seeking God," the end and focus of all Benedictine life, with its emphasis on listening, balance, focus, and ongoing conversion. It should be clear by now that Hildegard was convinced that a balanced life lived in the tension of opposites is possible only in and through the bright-burning understanding that has its origin and cause in Divine Love (*Caritas*). "Listen with the ears of your heart," St. Benedict advised. To what? To the presence and patterns of Love:

> I am also rationality, having the wind of the resounding Word (through which all creation was made), and I have breathed into all these things, so that there is nothing mortal in their natures, because I am Life itself. For I am the whole of life.... Every living thing is rooted in me. For rationality is the root, but the resounding Word flowers in it.
>
> Hence, since God is rational, how could he not be at work since all his work blossoms in man whom he made in his own image and likeness and in whom he expressed all creation according to fixed measure. For it was always the case throughout eternity that God wanted his work, man, to come into being. And when he finished the task, he gave man all the creatures so that he might work with them, just as God had made man his own work. (WM I, 2)

The third bridge into the territory of Hildegard's symbolic spirituality I suggested was the female experience as filter and lens. I have tried to give a taste of Hildegard's theology of Wisdom, of a fertility in interconnectedness she calls *viriditas*. Having experienced a profound affirmation by God of her identity as a woman, she filtered her visionary experiences of the Mystery of God through her specific female mode of consciousness. After she broke the shackles of her conditioning and fear, she expressed her experiences of the mystery in words and images that rang most true with her being as a woman. The term *viriditas*, fecundity of interrelated mutuality, points both to God's fecundity that desires embodiment in history and to the human potential to live lives of fecundity on many levels. I have proposed that this unusual word arose from the depth of this woman's psyche, from her willingness to live in the no-man's-land between received God-images and God's self-disclosure to her. The "gendered" experience on which I have focused shaped her God-images and also the way in which she spoke about the labor pains of the new creation.

Hildegard's writings abound with maternal imagery that delineates the relational, renewing work of *Caritas* in the world. A powerful symbolic image from a vision in *De operatione Dei* speaks clearly to the maternal aspect of *Caritas*. The entire cosmos, and the human being in its center, is imaged as a living organ in the heart or womb of God. God, the eternally alive One, embraces the cosmos with a fiery circle of Divine Love, the Cosmic Christ (see illumination 4, p. 80, above). Standing cruciform in the center, the human holds a gossamer net of rays that is connected to all the elements. The net or rays emerge from the mouth of this *Caritas*-figure, the Cosmic Christ: "From the primordial source of Divine Love, in whom the cosmic order rests, shines her exceedingly precise ordering of things. It comes to light in ever-new ways, holding and tending everything there is" (DW II, 46). The "exceedingly precise ordering of things" that connects all things shows another facet of the matrix of Love. It is the pattern of Love, made explicit in the life, death, and resurrection of Christ. This pattern, the pattern of *viriditas*, desires to become incarnate in a relational, unbroken web life. It is the pattern and power human discernment tries to discover and give birth to.

In a letter to Abbot Adam of the Ebrach monastery, Hildegard sees Divine Love as a beautiful girl whom all creatures call their sovereign lady, as the creative, fertile power in the womb of reality:

And I heard a voice saying to me: This girl that you see is Divine Love, and she has her dwelling place in eternity. For when God wished to create the world, He bent down in sweetest love, and He provided for all the necessary things, just as a father prepares the inheritance for his son. Thus it was that in great ardor He established all His works in order. Then all creation in its various kinds and forms acknowledged its Creator, for in the beginning divine love was the matrix from which He created all things, when He said, Let there be, and it was done [cf. Gen. 1:3]. Thus every creature was formed through divine love in the twinkling of an eye....

And all creatures name this girl sovereign lady because they all came forth from her — since she was the creator of all things from the beginning — just as also, the image on her breast shows that God dressed himself in humanity for mankind's sake. For when creation was fulfilled by God's commandment — just as He himself said: "Increase and multiply, and fill the earth" [Gen. 1:28] — the heat of the true sun descended like dew into the womb of the Virgin and made man from her flesh, just as also He formed Adam's flesh and blood from the mud of the earth. And the Virgin gave birth to Him immaculately.

But it was not fitting for divine love not to have wings. For when the creature began circling aimlessly about in the beginning, it wished to fly, despite its earthbound nature, and so it fell, but it was the wings of divine love that lifted it up. These wings were holy humility. For when horrible misjudgment laid Adam low, divinity kept a sharp eye on him so that he might not perish utterly in the fall but that divinity itself might redeem him in the holiness of humanity. These were wings of great power, for humility — which was the humanity of the Savior — raised up mankind who was lost, for divine love created man, but humility redeemed him. Hope is, as it were, the eye of divine love, celestial love its heart; and abstinence the link between the two. But faith is, as it were, the eye of humility; obedience its heart, and contempt for evil the link between the two. Divine love was in eternity, and, in the beginning of all sanctity, she brought forth all creatures without any mixture of evil, and she brought forth Adam and Eve from the immaculate earth. And just as the two of them brought forth the children of mankind, so too, those two virtues bring forth all the other virtues. (L 193–94)

Divine Love is the matrix not only of creation but also of redemption, Hildegard indicates. In her comments on 1 John 4:9–10 ("God's love was revealed among us in this way: God sent his only Son into the world so that we might live through him. In this is love, not that we loved God but that he loved us and sent his Son to be the atoning sacrifice for our sins"),

Hildegard says the following, a statement we have had cause to cite numerous times above:

> Through the fountain-fullness of the Word came the embrace of God's maternal love, which nourishes us into life, is our help in perils, and — as a most profound and gentle love — opens us for repentance. (SC II, 2, 4)

> The redeeming deed of Love did not originate with us. We did not understand it and were not capable of loving God for our salvation. Rather, God as creator and ruler so loved his people that for their redemption he sent his Son, the head and Savior of the faithful. He washed and cleansed our wounds. He is the source of the most delightful disposition from which all goods of salvation flow. (SC II, 2, 4)

If we return to the words of *Caritas* in *De operatione Dei*, the redemptive and empowering character of Divine Love is clarified further:

> But I am also of service since all living things take their radiance from me; and I am the life which remains the same through eternity, having neither beginning nor end; and the same life, working and moving itself is God and yet this life is one in three powers. And so Eternity is called the Father, the Word is called the Son and the breath that connects these two is called the Holy Spirit; just as God marked it in man in whom there are body, soul and rationality. (WM I, 2)

Caritas, Love, reveals itself as a Trinitarian energy pattern of ever-circling Love and response or, as Hildegard would say, embrace (*amplexio caritatis*). In Hildegard's unusual image of the Trinity as a flaming eye of love, whose pupil is a blessing sapphire-blue Christ figure (see illumination 6), Divine Love is symbolized as the very life of God ("the same life, working and moving itself is God and yet this life is one in three powers"). In *Scivias*, Hildegard writes:

> And I saw a blinding brightness and in this light a sapphire-blue figure all ablaze in a gentle glowing fire. And that bright light suffused the entire glowing fire, and the glowing fire suffused the blinding light and the blinding light and the

Illumination 6
The Trinity

glowing fire poured over the whole human figure so that the three formed one light in the power and brilliance of potential. And I again heard the Living Light speaking to me:

1. On the Perception of the Divine Mystery

The Divine Mystery is sensed in this way: In the clear perception and understanding of what this Fullness indicates, whose origin was never seen, which does not lack the most effective energy which flows from the sources of strength. If God were empty of his own vitality, what would his works be? They would obviously be in vain. Therefore one recognizes the originator in the completed works.

2. On the Three Persons

Therefore you see a *blinding brightness* which without the flaw of illusion, deficiency, or deception designates the Father; *and in this light the sapphire-blue figure of a human,* which without the law of hardness, of envy, or iniquity designates the Son. Begotten by the Father in eternity, and then in time, he became incarnate on earth in the flesh. The figure is completely *ablaze in a gentle glowing fire.* This fire, without any flaw of aridity, mortality or darkness, designates the Holy Spirit through whom the Only Begotten of God was conceived in the flesh and born by the Virgin in time, and poured out the light of true glory into the world. *And that bright light suffused the entire glowing fire and the blinding light and the glowing fire poured over the whole human figure so that the three formed one light in the power and brilliance of potential.* This means that...the Father, who signifies all measured justice, but not without the Son or the Holy Spirit; and the Holy Spirit, who kindles the hearts of the faithful, but not without the Father or the Son; and the Son, who is the plenitude of fecundity, but not without the Father or the Holy Spirit — are inseparable in the majesty of the Godhead. For the Father is not without the Son, nor the Son without the Father, and neither the Father nor the Son without the Holy Spirit, nor the Holy Spirit without them.... The Father, however, is revealed through the Son, the Son through creation, and the Holy Spirit through the Incarnate Son. (SC II, 2, 1–2)

God as the fullness of life-giving, clarifying, vivifying light for all that is was a powerful reality for Hildegard. She knew a God who became human to make us co-creators in creation, a God who, in the Holy Spirit, draws us into the power and patterns of Divine Love. Hildegard's Trinitarian image grounds the human nature in our relationship to God. As earlier chapters tried to show, the mystery of Christ's fecundity (*viriditas*) is not restricted to his role as redeemer from sin. His fecundity permeates all spheres of reality, the entire cosmos and history, time and eternity, the individual and the human community. *Viriditas*, the fecundity of mutual interrelatedness, which is the work of Christ and our task, is rooted in the Trinitarian mystery of continually moving and responding Love, which Hildegard symbolized in her unusual image of the Trinity.

Human choice involves us in the dynamic process of bringing the creative, dynamic fecundity of this Trinitarian Love into the here-and-now. The sapphire-blue blessing Christ figure is neither male nor female. Does it point to the cosmic dimension of the mystery of Christ and perhaps also to a cosmic dimension of our humanity, which grounds human identity in the relationship to God? Including this dimension in the definition of what it means to be human, then, would include a calling to become the earth in which the seeds of Christ's fecundity can bear fruit. Hildegard's unusual Trinitarian image is yet another one of her powerful symbols that not only points to a deep theological truth but also calls us out of the realm of aridity into creative fecundity and mutuality in the entire web of life.

Love, the matrix of creation, redemption, and brightburning understanding, is brooding over the world like a mother hen tending her chicks. Hildegard's specific focus holds implications for our century. By showing us many facets and modes of Love's reality and presence, Hildegard can help us to break through all the conditioning that restricts understanding this mystery at the core of all reality. We are capable of reaching such an understanding because Love accompanies us as the midwife who stays with us in the labor pains of the "new creation."

Hildegard's visionary, contemplative theology differs not only from abstract theology but also from the monastic theology of the monks. She filtered her experiences of the Living

Light through her female experience and mode of consciousness and gradually found words and symbols that reveal a
woman's ways of perception. In the grand sweep of her symbolic universe, which is traditional yet new, one theological
symbol stands out: *viriditas*, the fecundity of mutual interrelatedness. Hildegard, who was proposed as the third female
"Doctor of the Church," redeems woman's identity and experience as the image and likeness of God, thus overcoming the
marginalization of women's experience as revealing the divine.
Being a woman, being fertile, being capable of giving life, is
not a polluted or second-class state, but rather a mode of being
human that points to the many modes of our participation in
divine fecundity that can and should be exercised.

Hildegard's focus and work redeem the identity of matter
and of the historical process when she speaks of them as being
sustained and empowered by the presence of God's fecundity
and by *Caritas*. The whole world is the cosmic body of Christ,
whose work is *viriditas*. When she tells us about the mothering
nature of Divine Love, she helps us to overcome the barrenness of naming the experience of the Divine Mystery in solely
male terms.

As our earth is threatened, becoming a wasteland, as people
and nations hide ever more in self-protective patterns of isolation, as fear constricts so many hearts, let us listen to Hildegard
of Bingen. She was a prophet who knew both the heartbeat of
God's Love and the powers that oppose it and create a world
filled with aridity and fear. She challenges us across the centuries to find both that Love and those powers in the depths
of our own hearts. She calls us to a change of mind and heart,
to awe, to repentance, to good works and courageous actions.
These need to have their source in the bright-burning understanding of Love that empowers discernment. When the depth
of aridity, the depth of the human ability to respond, and the
depth of Divine Love are keenly known, then they become
praise and action — they become *viriditas*.

Chronology

1098   Hildegard is born in Bermersheim as the tenth child of a noble family.

1106   Hildegard is given into the care of the anchoress Jutta von Sponheim. The anchorage is attached to the Benedictine monastery on Mount Disiboden.

1136   After Jutta's death, Hildegard is elected abbess.

1141   Hildegard receives the prophetic call vision that tells her to write and proclaim what she "sees" and "hears." With the help of the monk Volmar, her secretary and friend, and the nun Richardis, she begins the writing of *Scivias* (Know the Ways of God).

1147–48   At the synod in Trier, Pope Eugenius III reads to the assembled bishops from Hildegard's writings, affirms her visionary gifts, and urges her to write her visions down.

1150   Hildegard's own convent is founded on the Rupertsberg, a mountain near Bingen, after a vision commands her to do so. The monks of the Disibodenberg monastery strongly object, but Hildegard overcomes all obstacles.

1151   Hildegard completes the writing of *Scivias*

1151–58   Hildegard composes a natural history, *Physica,* and a medical book, *Causae et curae.*

1155   Hildegard demands and then in 1158 receives a legal separation of her own foundation from the Disibodenberg monastery.

1158–63   *Liber vitae meritorum* (The Book of Life's Merits) is written. It depicts thirty-five virtues, or powers of God, confronting an equal number of vices.

1158–61   Hildegard makes her first extensive preaching journey, visiting Mainz, Würzburg, Wertheim, Ebrach,
Kitzingen, and Bamberg. Although in ill-health, she
preaches in cathedrals and market squares.

1159   Hildegard corresponds with Emperor Barbarossa re-
garding a schism.

1160   Hildegard makes her second preaching journey along
the River Mosel. On Pentecost, she openly preaches
in Trier.

1161–63   She undertakes a third preaching journey, along the
Rhine River.

1163   Hildegard begins her last great visionary book, *Liber
divinorum operum* (The Book of Divine Works), a cosmology. It is completed in 1173–74.

Ca. 1165   A daughter convent is founded in Eibingen near
Ruedesheim. To visit, Hildegard crosses the Rhine
twice weekly.

1170   Hildegard undertakes a fourth preaching journey,
visiting various abbeys.

1174–75   Her secretary, Gottfried, writes book 1 of *Vita*, her
biography.

1175   Wibert of Gembloux writes Hildegard. She responds
with the famous letter describing the mode of her
visions.

1178   An excommunicated nobleman is buried in the convent cemetery. Ecclesial authorities demand his re-
moval from sacred ground. Convinced that this man
had been reconciled to God through confession, Hildegard refuses. An Interdict is imposed, prohibiting
all liturgical services.

1179   The Interdict is removed.

1179   Hildegard dies on September 17.

Select Bibliography

HILDEGARD'S WORKS

Sources of originals: PL = J. P. Migne, ed., *Sanctae Hildegardis abbatissae Opera omnia*, in *Patrologiae cursus completus: Series latina* 197 (Paris, 1855); includes *Vita S. Hildegardis, 145 Epistolae, Scivias, Liber divinorum Operum, Physica,* and several short works. PI = J. P. Pitra, ed., *Analecta S. Hildegardis*, vol. 8 of *Analecta sacra* (Monte Cassino, 1882); includes *Liber vitae meritorum, Expositiones evangeliorum, 145 Epistolae* not contained in Migne, and fragments.

Scivias *(in PL)*

Führkötter, Adelgundis, and Angela Carnevalis, eds., *Hildegardis — Scivias: Corpus Christianorum: Continuatio mediaevalis.* Corpus Christianorum: Continuatio mediaevalis, vols. 43–43a. Turnhout, Belgium: Brepols, 1978. Critical edition.

Hart, Columba, and Jane Bishop, trans. *Hildegard of Bingen: Scivias.* Classics of Western Spirituality. New York: Paulist Press, 1990. Introduction by Barbara Newman, preface by Caroline Walker Bynum. With Black and white illustrations.

Hozeski, Bruce, trans. *Hildegard of Bingen's "Scivias."* Santa Fe: Bear and Company, 1986. Abridged translation.

Storch, Walburga, trans. *Hildegard von Bingen, Scivias — Wisse die Wege: Eine Schau von Gott und Mensch in Schöpfung und Zeit.* Freiburg im Breisgau: Herder, 1992.

Liber Divinorum Operum *(The Book of Divine Works) (in PL)*

Fox, Matthew, ed. and trans. *Hildegard of Bingen's Book of Divine Works, with Letters and Songs.* Santa Fe: Bear and Company, 1987. Abridged translation.

Schipperges, Heinrich, trans. *Der Mensch in der Verantwortung — Das Buch: De operatione Dei.* Salzburg: Otto Müller Verlag, 1965. Includes color plates from the illuminated Lucca manuscript.

Liber Vitae Meritorum *(Book of Life's Merits) (in PI)*

Schipperges, Heinrich, trans. *Der Mensch in der Verantwortung — Liber vitae meritorum.* Salzburg: Otto Müller Verlag, 1972.

Liber subtilitarum diversarum naturarum creaturam: Liber simplicis medicinae/physica *(Book of Simple Medicine or Natural History) (in PL)*

Riether, P., trans. *Naturkunde: Das Buch von dem inneren Wesen der verschiedenen Naturen der Schöpfung — Physica.* Salzburg: Otto Müller Verlag, 1959.

Schipperges, Heinrich, trans. *Heilkunde: Das Buch von dem inneren Wesen der verschiedenen Naturen der Schöpfung — Physica.* Salzburg: Otto Müller Verlag, 1959.

Liber compositae medicinae/causae et curae *(Causes and Cures)*

Kaiser, Paul, trans. *Hildegardis Causae et curae.* Leipzig: Teubner, 1903.

Schulz, Hugo, and Ferd. Sauerbruch, trans. *Ursachen und Behandlungen der Krankheiten (Causae et curae).* Heidelberg: Karl Haug Verlag, 1955.

Symphonia harmoniae caelestium revelationum *(Symphony of the Harmony of Celestial Revelations) (in PI)*

Barth, Prudentia, Immaculata Ritscher, and Joseph Schmidt-Görg, trans. *Hildegard von Bingen: Lieder.* Salzburg: Otto Müller Verlag, 1969. Text translation and music of *Symphonia* and *Ordo virtutum.*

Newman, Barbara, ed. and trans. *Saint Hildegard of Bingen: Symphonia.* Ithaca, N.Y.: Cornell University Press, 1988. Critical edition with English translations and commentary.

Ordo virtutum *(Play of the Virtues) (in PI)*

Davidson, Audrey, ed. *Hildegard von Bingen, "Ordo Virtutum."* Kalamazoo, Mich.: Medieval Institute Publications, 1985. Performance edition with music.

Dronke, Peter, ed. *Poetic Individuality of the Middle Ages.* Oxford: Oxford University Press, 1970. Critical edition.

Explanatio regulae s. benedicti *(Commentary on the Rule of St. Benedict) (in PL)*

Feiss, Hugh, trans. *Explanation of the Rule of St. Benedict.* Toronto: Peregrina, 1990.

Epistolae *(Letters) (in PI and PL)*

Baird, Joseph L., and Radd Ehrman, trans. *The Letters of Hildegard von Bingen.* Volume 1. New York: Oxford University Press, 1994.

Dronke, Peter, ed. and trans. *Women Writers of the Middle Ages.* Cambridge: Cambridge University Press, 1984. Latin text and English translation of some letters.

Führkötter, Adelgundis, ed. and trans. *Hildegard von Bingen: Briefwechsel.* Salzburg: Otto Müller Verlag, 1965. German translation of selected letters with introduction and commentary.

BIOGRAPHICAL WORK BY HILDEGARD'S CONTEMPORARIES

Vita sanctae Hildegardis *(Life of St. Hildegard), by Godfrey and Theodoric (in PL)*

Führkötter, Adelgundis, trans. *Das Leben der hl. Hildegard von Bingen — Vita S. Hildegardis.* Salzburg: Otto Müller Verlag, 1980.

STUDIES

Betz, Otto. *Hildegard von Bingen: Gestalt und Werk.* Munich: Kösel Verlag, 1996.

Bonn, Caecilia. *Der Mensch in der Entscheidung: Gedanken zur Ganzheitlichen Schau Hildegard's von Bingen.* Eibingen: Abtei St. Hildegard, 1986.

————. "Gottesvergessenheit führt ins Chaos." *Festansprache* 17 (September 1993).

————. *Weg zu Gott: Hildegard von Bingen-Lehrmeisterin des geistlichen Lebens.* Eltville am Rhein: G.A. Walter's Druckerei. Contains four lectures.

Bowie, Fiona, and Oliver Davies, eds., Robert Carver, trans. *Hildegard of Bingen: Mystical Writings.* Crossroad Spiritual Classics. New York: Crossroad, 1990.

Brück, Anton, ed. *Hildegard von Bingen, 1179–1979: Festschrift zum 800. Todestag der Heiligen.* Mainz: Selbstverlag der Gesellschaft für Mittelrheinische Kirchengeschichte, 1979.

Craine, Renate. "Hildegard of Bingen: 'The Earth Hungers for the Fullness of Justice.'" *Cistercian Studies* 2 (1991): 120–26.

Dronke, Peter. "Problemata Hildegardiana." *Mittellateinisches Jahrbuch* 16 (1981): 97–131.

Flanagan, Sabina. *Hildegard von Bingen: A Visionary Life.* New York: Routledge, 1989.

Fox, Matthew. *Illuminations of Hildegard of Bingen.* Santa Fe: Bear and Company, 1985. Contains illuminations and creation-centered interpretation of Hildegard's text.

Führkötter, Adelgundis. *Hildegard von Bingen: Ruf in die Zeit.* Cologne: Rheinland Verlag, 1985.

————, ed. *Kosmos und Mensch.* Mainz: Verlag der Gesellschaft für Mittelrheinische Kirchengeschichte, 1987.

Gronau, Eduard. *Hildegard von Bingen 1098–1179: Prophetische Lehrerin der Kirche an der Schwelle und am Ende der Neuzeit.* Stein am Rhein: Christiana Verlag, 1985.

Lachman, Barbara. *A Journal of Hildegard of Bingen: A Novel.* New York: Bell Tower, 1993.

Lauter, Werner. *Hildegard Bibliographie.* Vol. 1. Alzey: Verlag der Rheinhessischen Druckerwerkstätte, 1970. Vol. 2, 1984.

Meier, Christel. "Die Bedeutung der Farben in der Welt Hildegards von Bingen." *Frühmittelalterliche Studien* 6 (1972): 251–355.

Newman, Barbara. "Hildegard of Bingen: Visions and Validation." *Church History* 54 (1985): 163–75.

————. *Sister of Wisdom: St. Hildegard's Theology of the Feminine.* Berkeley: University of California Press, 1987.

Ohanneson, Joan. *Scarlet Music: Hildegard von Bingen, a Novel.* New York: Crossroad, 1997.

Schipperges, Heinrich. *Hildegard von Bingen: Ein Zeichen für unsere Zeit.* Frankfurt: Josef Knecht, 1981.

————. *Die Welt der Engel bei Hildegard von Bingen.* 2d ed. Salzburg: Otto Müller Verlag, 1979.

————, ed. *Hildegard von Bingen: Gott sehen.* Munich: Piper, 1985.

Schipperges, Heinrich, and Caecilia Bonn. *Hildegard von Bingen und ihre Impulse für die moderne Welt.* Eibingen: Abtei St. Hildegard, 1984.

Schmidt, Margot, ed. *Tiefe des Gotteswissens — Schönheit der Sprachgestalt bei Hildegard von Bingen.* Intenationales Symposium in der Katholischen Akademie St. Rabanus Maurus Wiesbaden-Naurod, September 9 to 12, 1994. Stuttgart: Friedrich Frommann Verlag/ Günter Holzboog, 1995.

Sölle, Dorothee. *O Grün des Finger Gottes: Die Meditationen der Hildegard von Bingen.* Wuppertal: Peter Hammer Verlag, 1989.

Strehlow, Wighart, and Gottfried Hertzka. *Hildegard of Bingen's Medicine.* Santa Fe: Bear and Company, 1988.

Strickerschmidt, Hildegard. *Heilige Hildegard: Heilung an Leib und Seele.* Augsburg: Pattloch Verlag, 1993.

Ulanov, Ann Belford. *The Wisdom of the Psyche.* Cambridge, Mass.: Cowley Publications, 1988.